Easy Progr: for the Oric-1

Ian Stewart
Mathematics Institute, University of Warwick

Robin Jones
Computer Unit, South Kent College of Technology

Shiva Publishing Limited

SHIVA PUBLISHING LIMITED
4 Church Lane, Nantwich, Cheshire CW5 5RQ, England

ISBN 0 906812 43 7

Cover photograph of the Oric-1 courtesy of Oric Products International Ltd.

To James and Christopher:
One day, all this will be . . .
completely different.

Typeset by Gilbert Composing Services, Leighton Buzzard
and printed by Devon Print Group, Exeter.

Contents

Introduction

Tangerine's Oric-1 microcomputer offers sound, colour and high resolution graphics at a remarkably modest price. The aim of this book is to make the basic features of the Oric accessible to the newcomer to computing, and to provide useful information for the more experienced user who is transferring from another machine.

When you buy your Oric, you get a comprehensive *User Manual* with it. So why buy a book?

Since you're reading this, you probably have an idea of the answer. It's difficult for a Manual to be both comprehensive *and* comprehensible. Manuals have to be all things to all people, and they tend to lack the space needed for proper and careful explanations in the kind of detail that a beginner may need.

In addition, some of the more exciting features, such as sound and colour, are a little tricky to use effectively: a few general hints and sample programs can go a long way, helping you to use the Oric's capabilities to the full.

So what's on offer here?

First, a reasonably thorough description of the fundamentals of BASIC, the Oric's native tongue. We've concentrated on the commands that are most important for a beginner: when you've mastered these, the *Manual* will look a great deal less daunting and you'll be able to fill in some of the gaps. We've deliberately avoided anything beyond the simplest mathematics: you can go a long way without it! Each command or group of commands is illustrated by sample programs, ranging from short test programs to more lengthy games and utility programs. These are not intended to be masterpieces of awe-inspiring power and beauty, because the listings for *really* fancy programs can become so long that nobody would have the energy to type them in. They *are* intended to illustrate how a little attention to detail can greatly improve the looks and function of a program, and to show you what the machine can be made to do with a reasonable amount of effort.

Each chapter also includes one or more projects for you to tackle. *Answers are provided,* so you can use the projects to test your understanding *and* to augment it.

The sample programs can be copied and run without having to understand how they work, and each is accompanied by an explanation of how it achieves its effects.

Second, we've included a series of chapters on *debugging:* how to find errors in programs and correct them. If you really want to write your own programs, these techniques are indispensible. Yet very few books bother to tell you about them. (The trick is seeing the wood for the trees. For example Oric has a *trace* command that will print out program lines as they are carried out; but if you list *every* line, the screen will fill up so fast you'll never see what's going on. So you need to be selective.)

Third, we've described a few useful techniques for writing programs that are easy to understand and easy to get working. To begin with you'll be happy if a program produces the right result, however messy or clumsy it may be; and that's fair enough. But for longer and more sophisticated programs, a readable structure is important.

Fourth, we've included information on the way the Oric works, which is not listed in the *Manual* in sufficient detail: CTRL keys, alternate characters, using the screen editor . . . .

Fifth, we provide much more explanation of how to use the sound and colour facilities: musical harmony, low and high resolution graphics, the use of colour commands (serial attributes) in both low resolution and high resolution (in which colour commands must be 'poked to the screen'), moving graphics and keyboard control.

The Oric is a versatile beast; but it takes a little effort to get the best out of it. This book certainly doesn't exhaust the possibilities—it would take a great many books to do *that*—but it should help you get properly started.

After all, the hardest part is getting off the ground.

NOTE FOR EXPERTS

As we've just said, this is a book for first-time users: it's not written for experts. In particular, the *simplest* way to achieve a desired result is not always the most *efficient*. So if we sometimes appear to be doing things in a clumsy way, we probably are. However, it makes good sense to learn to walk before you run; and to learn the simple features before moving on to sophisticated and more powerful ones.

Similarly, don't expect the program-listings to be highly polished production versions with arcade-quality graphics, performing miracles of computation at breathtaking speed. The aim here is to produce simple listings that the reader can (a) type in in a finite time, and (b) work through and *understand*. The really fancy stuff should come later.

Note for Grammarians and Pedants

Some half-dozen books back, we decided that we ought to refer to ourselves collectively, as 'I'. It's perhaps a trifle unorthodox, but it's very convenient because we occasionally have to relate personal experiences. "As we said to our wife this morning . . . "—no, that doesn't sound right. So 'I' is some sort of composite of us both. 'We' henceforth means 'I and the reader'.

First, how to set up the hardware.
You've probably managed this already,
but if not, a few hints may help.

1 Up and Running

If you've ever connected up a TV game, or another breed of home computer, to your television set, you'll have no trouble setting up the Oric. But in case you haven't, I'll start with a quick run through the procedure.

When you unpacked your Oric you should have found:

1. The computer.
2. The power-pack, like an overfed electric plug with a long lead ending at a much tinier plug.
3. The TV connection cable, a *single* coaxial cable with a coaxial connector on each end.
4. The cassette connection cable, a *double* cable with more complicated plugs that have three pins inside a round outside bit (technically known as three-pin DIN plugs).
5. The book *Oric-1: BASIC Programming Manual* (which I'll shorten to *Manual* from now on).

Before connecting everything together, it's a good idea to decide on a civilized layout. Unless you're using a spare TV set, the Oric is going to have to live somewhere near the usual place you put the TV. On the floor is *not* a good idea; you'll risk treading on the Oric and damaging it. Worse, you'll end up with pins-and-needles from sitting cramped up. So get a table, something like a coffee-table, and a chair, and place them by the TV.

The Oric has a keyboard on top and a lot of sockets in the back. Plug the lead from the power-pack into the leftmost socket (as viewed from the front) which is a hole with a central pin, next to two long sockets with parallel pairs of pins. Plug the 'male' end of the TV cable into the rightmost socket (viewed from the front). Plug the other end of the TV cable into the TV, where the aerial connection usually goes. (This will be marked UHF on the TV.)

Incidentally, the Oric will work perfectly well on a black-and-white TV; but of course you won't be able to use its colour facilities.

Some TVs have a numbered rotating dial to set the channels. If yours is like this, set the dial to Channel 36.

If not, you'll have six or eight preset buttons to select channels. On most sets numbers 1, 2, 3 give BBC-1, BBC-2 and ITV. (And, these days, 4 gets Channel 4). In actual fact any button can be adjusted to set it to any channel, so your TV may not follow the usual pattern. Either way, select a number that you don't use for anything, say number six, and press that button.

Now plug the power-pack directly into the mains. Switch on the TV and the Oric. If you've remembered to switch on at the socket, you'll hear the Oric buzzing at you. This is perfectly normal and a sign of good health, like wet noses on dogs, so don't worry.

At this stage you will probably see just a random screenful of 'snow' because you haven't tuned the channel selector yet. Somewhere on the TV is a set of six (or eight) little rotating dials that do this. Often it's concealed behind a little panel. If you've never noticed it have a good search: you'll be surprised! Sometimes the maker's name flaps down, sometimes a whole section pops out if you give it a push in the right place. Having found it, adjust dial number six (your chosen channel number) until the screen displays a message. You'll probably have to turn the dial several times and you may need to reverse direction if turning it one way doesn't seem to be working.

Figure 1.1   A tidy layout is recommended.

Even if you have a numbered dial and have found channel 36, a little fine-tuning may be needed to get the best picture. You may also need to adjust the brightness and contrast controls, and the colour setting (and just occasionally horizontal and vertical hold).

What you are looking for is a clear white screen with a black border displaying the message:

ORIC EXTENDED BASIC V1.Ø

© 1983 TANGERINE

47870 BYTES FREE

Ready

(That's for the current 48K machine: the numbers in the message may be different depending on which version of the computer you've got.)

Sometimes you don't get this: instead you get a picture made up of black and white blocks and stripes, possibly flickering quite rapidly. If so, switch off at the mains for a few seconds and switch on again: the Oric will then reset itself correctly and display its message.

Once you have found this, the computer is ready for action. If you can't get anything, check that everything is switched on and connected properly, and that the plugs are firmly in their sockets; then try adjusting the tuning again. When you get close to the right place you'll see flickering lines on the screen, dimly visible through the snow. If you still can't pick up the message after tracking from one end of the tuning range to the other, either you're turning the wrong dial or something isn't quite right. If you're at all handy, take a look at the connections on the leads and see whether any wires have come adrift, and/or check the continuity of the leads and test for short circuits using a battery and a torch bulb. If you still get nowhere, contact the shop that you bought the Oric from. Computer hardware is very reliable, but it *can* sometimes go wrong.

CASSETTE RECORDERS

At a later stage you will wish to connect up a cassette recorder to your Oric to load or save programs on tape. But for the moment we won't try to do this. See Chapter 13 if you particularly want to know how, or if you're having problems with the Oric demonstration tape.

A DISCREET WORD OF ADVICE

It is just possible that certain members of your household are not as enamoured of the Oric as you are. They will conceal these feelings successfully, until the day they switch on the TV to watch Dallas and get a multicoloured hissing snowstorm. So, when you have finished using the Oric, *restore the TV to its normal settings and check that it's tuned correctly.*

What do those keys on the Oric do?
If you push them at random, not a lot!
But at least that way you'll get a
good feel for:

2 The Keyboard

The Oric keyboard is just like a typewriter keyboard, and the letters are arranged in the same 'qwerty' pattern. Basically this is a stupid arrangement that goes back to the early days of typewriters when keys often jammed; but it has become so utterly standardized that we all have to learn to live with it.

As well as the letters and numbers there are keys marked ESC, CTRL, and SHIFT down the left side; DEL, RETURN, SHIFT down the right side; and along the bottom is a long bar flanked by two pairs of keys with arrows. This is the *space bar,* just as on a typewriter; and the arrow keys are *cursor control keys* (see later).

The first step is to get the feel of the keyboard. It takes a while to get used to all the things that the keyboard can be made to do, but the one thing you can't do by typing is damage the machine. So feel free to experiment: if you end up stuck with some weird effect (which is possible) just switch off and then on again (or see RESET on page 8).

Assuming you've just switched on, you'll have the copyright message, and a flashing square called a *cursor.* This controls whereabouts on the TV screen things get printed. Press the key marked 'A'; you'll see an A appear where the cursor was, and the cursor itself moves one space right. You'll also hear a fairly high-pitched bleep, which lets you know that the computer has reacted to the key-press—very useful when you're typing in a long program and don't want to look at the screen too often to check.

Press other keys. To make life easy, stick to the ones with letters and numbers on for a while. Hold a key down for a second or two: you'll find it produces the same letter over and over again. This is called *auto-repeat.* After you've filled two lines of screen the computer will give a sharp, resounding PING! This just means you've exceeded the size limit for messages; ignore it for the moment.

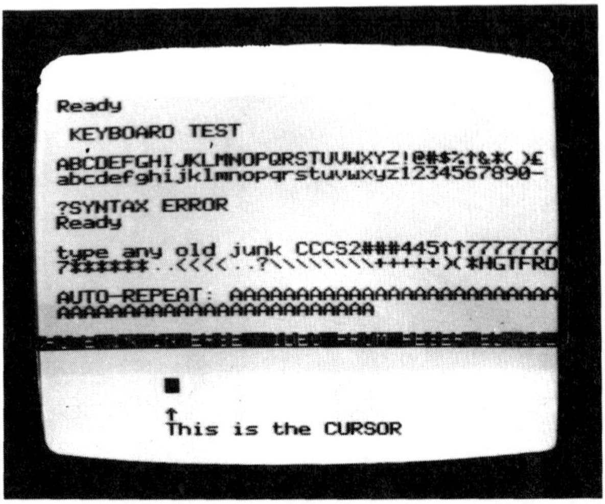

Figure 2.1   Some of the features available from the keyboard.

6

SHIFT

The two keys marked SHIFT both have the same effect, which is just as on a typewriter. If you hold down a SHIFT key with one hand and press another key, you get *upper case* characters. For instance, hold down SHIFT and hit key '5'. What you see is a percentage sign '%'; and if you look at the key you'll see that it has the '%' marked over the top of the '5'. If a key has two symbols written by it, SHIFT produces the upper one, and no SHIFT the lower.

The letter keys A–Z are marked only in capitals; and at the moment that's all they'll produce, either with or without SHIFT. But there *is* a way to get lower case letters a–z, which I'll explain later.

RETURN

In a way, this is the most important key on the computer. When you press it, whatever you've typed is shovelled into the computer's memory. Until that point, all the computer does is display things on the screen; but when you hit RETURN it will *act* on them.

Type in some rubbish like:

AAABBBBB%%67QJ

and then hit RETURN. What you get is a message:

? SYNTAX ERROR

Ready

This means that the Oric has received your instruction, but (not surprisingly) doesn't understand it. If you type in a more meaningful message it will carry it out. For example, press RETURN (to get rid of any junk) and then type:

EXPLODE   (and hit RETURN)

It does! At least, it produces an explosion *sound.* So *that* message made sense, and was acted upon.

SPACE BAR

The long space bar at the bottom produces blank spaces, just as on a typewriter. These are useful for leaving gaps between words, and for getting tidy screen displays.

CURSOR KEYS

The keys with arrows on move the flashing cursor around. Try them out. The *left* (←) and *right* (→) arrows move the cursor along a row; the *up* (↑) and *down* (↓) move it vertically. If you try to go off the edge then two different things can happen:

1. For → and ← : the cursor reappears on the other side of the screen, but one row lower (higher).
2. For ↑ and ↓: the cursor stays in place but the rest of the screen *scrolls.* That is, the symbols on the screen move up (like a piece of paper in a typewriter does when you go on to a new line) or down, depending on which arrow you've used.

Unlike a piece of paper, anything that scrolls off screen is lost: if you scroll back again, it is replaced by blanks.

DEL

This is the *delete* key, and it acts as an eraser. If you hit DEL then the cursor moves *back* a space, and rubs one character out. This is useful for correcting mistakes.

RESET

This 'key' isn't on the top of the Oric: it's hidden away underneath. There's a square hole. When you poke a pencil through this and push the button inside the machine, it will *reset* to its normal state. For instance, fill the screen with junk, and now RESET. You'll find the screen has cleared, the cursor is back at top left, and you're ready for action.

Figure 2.2   The RESET button lives inside this hole. Use a pencil to operate it.

RESET gives you a 'warm start' if you have a program in memory and something untoward occurs. It gets the the computer back into a 'ready-to-run' state, and unlike switching off the power, does not clear the contents of memory. So, if you get stuck in an endless loop, or you accidentally put the display out of synch, RESET!

CTRL

This stands for CONTROL, and I've left it towards the end because it's a real Pandora's box. If you hold down CTRL and press another key, all kinds of things can happen.

For instance, press CTRL and 'G'. There, that startled you, didn't it? You got that PING again. That's all CTRL/G does: it pings. CTRL/L clears the screen completely: try it.

If you press CTRL/T and start typing letters A–Z, you'll find they now come out in *lower* case, as a–z. (What happens if you now type SHIFT/A, etc.?)

To get out of this state, press CTRL/T again. You should see a message:

CAPS

at top right of screen; and now the shift has no effect on letters. (Effectively, this makes CTRL/T a *CAPS LOCK* key; note that it does not affect the top row of numbered keys, which still respond to SHIFT. The reason for having this facility is that all programs must be written in capitals, so you want the caps lock *on* in these circumstances.)

If you press CTRL/T repeatedly, the message CAPS appears and then disappears again. This is what the *Manual* means by *toggle action*: one press switches on, another off, the next on, and so on. Most of the CTRL keys toggle like this.

One useful key for distraught mums is CTRL/F, which cuts out the keyboard bleep (which is too loud for my tastes). If your keyboard won't bleep, try hitting CTRL/F in case you've accidentally toggled it off and need to toggle on again . . . .

There are lots of more esoteric CTRL keys: see Appendix 1, and experiment.

ESC

I mention this only for completeness: you probably won't need to use it, but experimenting may have left you with the impression that it does nothing at all. Actually it lets you send attributes (see Chapter 12) to the cursor position. For an example, position the cursor near the middle of the screen using the arrow keys, hit ESC, and then hit 'T'. A blue stripe will appear. The attribute code (Chapter 12) corresponds to the position of 'T' in the alphabet. The control keys CTRL/[and CTRL/Z also have this effect, which the *Manual* calls 'Escape Character Routine'.

SPACES

Spaces cause problems in program listings, because they're blank! In this book I'll adopt a convention to show spaces when they're important. Instead of printing a blank, I'll print the symbol:

∇

This is *not* available on the keyboard, so there should be no confusion. For example, I might write:

10   PRINT "STEWART∇AND∇JONES"

or

20   PRINT "A$\nabla$$\nabla$B$\nabla$$\nabla$C$\nabla$$\nabla$D"

If it's *obvious* where a space ought to go, I won't necessarily show it as a ∇ symbol.

A program is just a series of instructions, that are stored, to be carried out later. But first, you can try giving the commands direct from the keyboard.

3 Direct Commands

When you give the computer an instruction from the keyboard, so that it carries it out immediately the RETURN key is pressed, you are using it in *immediate* or *direct mode*. ('Mode' is computer jargon, and it would mean the 'state of mind' of the computer—if it had a mind. Hence the joke in a computer magazine that in a certain series of television programmes the presenter appeared to be functioning throughout in 'astonishment mode'.) There is another, *deferred mode,* in which the command is stored in memory and carried out later on. In fact a whole list of such commands is usually stored, forming a *program.* (The American spelling is standard in the industry and helps distinguish the technical term from the usual word 'programme', although the English version gets used a lot nowadays too.) I discuss programs in Chapter 4; for now, I'll function in immediate mode.

An Oric in immediate mode makes an impressive calculator, as well as a typewriter. Try this:

PRINT 2 + 2

(and then RETURN). You'll see the answer, 4, on the screen. Well, maybe *that* isn't impressive; but if you ask it to:

PRINT 12345678 + 87654321

it gives you 99999999 just as quickly.

Project 1

Get the computer to work out:

(a) 7 + 4
(b) 17 + 41
(c) 5 + 16
(d) 15123 + 97784

The Oric can also do subtraction:

PRINT 11 − 5

PRINT 77 − 3

PRINT 55555 − 22222

and so on.

For multiplication you must use the asterisk * instead of the usual multiplication sign × (because programmers confuse this with the letter X). Try:

PRINT 2 * 2

PRINT 2 * 3

PRINT 5 * 5

PRINT 99 * 77

Finally I'll mention division: for this the symbol / is used, rather than ÷. So to divide 24 by 3 you must ask for:

PRINT 24/3

and to divide 777 by 7:

PRINT 777/7

As well as whole numbers like these, the Oric can handle decimals like 27.342, and negative numbers like −99 or −27.342. It can also carry out a variety of mathematical calculations besides the arithmetical operations of addition, subtraction, multiplication and division. On the whole these refinements will not be required in this book.

Project 2

Try these commands out in immediate mode. What happens?

(a) ZAP
(b) PLOT 10, 10, 20
(c) PRINT "2 + 2"
(d) PRINT "ORIC"
(e) PRINT "ORIC" BACKWARDS
(f) PRINT "BACKWARDS"
(g) PRINT BACKWARDS
(h) PING
(i) DROP DEAD
(j) PLOT 5, 5, 17
(k) SOUND 1, 200, 3   (Use CTRL/C to stop this!)
(l) PAPER 4

A FEEBLE EXCUSE

Once you're happy with the keyboard, you'll be able to type in a command, or an entire program, and make it work, without having to understand any of the instructions in it.* You can even 'borrow' listings from books and magazines. *This is perfectly normal,* and you shouldn't feel guilty about it: everybody feels the urge from time to time. And it helps you to stay interested and to build confidence. (Like all good things, it shouldn't be overdone. If the Government's Information Technology year does nothing except produce a generation of people who can copy somebody else's software but not write their own, it might have been better to spend the money on a subsidy to Channel 4.)

* You just have, in Project 2.

Sometimes, when demonstrating a particular BASIC command, especially early on when we don't know very many, it would be nice to make use of a command that *hasn't been explained yet*. And that's precisely what I'm going to do if I feel it's appropriate.

So don't throw up your hands in horror and start moaning that the-silly-blighter-hasn't-told-us-about-that-yet: just grit your teeth, key the command in regardless, and observe the effect. It's there for your own good.

That's my excuse, anyway.

ANSWERS

Project 1

(a)	PRINT 7 + 4	(giving 11)
(b)	PRINT 17 + 41	(giving 58)
(c)	PRINT 5 + 16	(giving 21)
(d)	PRINT 15123 + 97784	(giving 112907)

Project 2

(a) Sound effect.
(b) Blue stripe.
(c) 2 + 2 appears on the screen, but it doesn't give the result, 4.
(d) ORIC appears on screen.
(e) ORIC0 appears on screen. (Why? It thinks BACKWARDS is a variable, equal to 0. See Chapter 6.)
(f) BACKWARDS appears on screen.
(g) 0 appears on screen. (Reason as in (e).)
(h) Sound effect.
(i) ?SYNTAX ERROR.
(j) Red stripe.
(k) Continuous tone, only stopping if you hit CTRL/C or switch off.
(l) Screen turns blue.

The way to get the computer to do what you want is to assemble the necessary instructions in a systematic list.

4 Programs

A *program* is a series of instructions for the computer to carry out. It's very like a recipe in a cookery book:

Take two eggs

Break them into a pan

Whisk them for 20 seconds

Add 2 kg tapioca

Add 4 cans of baked beans

and so forth. But a computer program has to be written in a very precise language.
Here is a simple program.

    10   PRINT "HELLO!";

    20   GOTO 10

You can type this into your computer. First, type NEW and hit RETURN—this will remove any remnants of previous programs. *ALWAYS do this before typing in a new program.* Then type in the first line:

    10   PRINT "HELLO!";

and RETURN. Because the instruction starts with a *number*, here 10, the computer treats it in deferred mode: it stores it away ready to carry it out when told to. Now type in:

    20   GOTO 10

plus RETURN. Don't worry about what any of this mumbo-jumbo *means* for the moment.

That's got it into memory, but how do we tell the computer to *execute* it (as the jargon goes)? We input the command:

    RUN

(plus RETURN, of course—I'm going to start omitting mention of that, but I'll expect you to hit RETURN at the end of each 'line' of a program and each instruction in immediate mode).

Assuming you've copied it out exactly as listed, all hell(o) will break loose. The word 'HELLO!' will appear all over the screen, moving around at high speed in a frenzied sort of way. And it will keep on doing it forever, unless you stop it. But how?

BREAK

To interrupt the machine in its deliberations (for example if you think it's got stuck because of a program bug) you just press:

CTRL/C   (that is, the CTRL key *and* the C key)

and it will (fairly) promptly stop, with a message:

BREAK IN 294   (or whatever line it had reached)

Ready

When you break the program above using CTRL/C, you'll get a BREAK message, usually referring to line 10 (because that line takes much longer to execute) but sometimes to line 20 (if you just hit the right timing). You can always use CTRL/C to stop a program if it seems to have got stuck or is doing something wrong.

CONT

To start up after a CTRL/C, you can use the command:

CONT

(short for 'continue'). Try it now: away she goes again!

WHAT'S GOING ON?

In a BASIC program, every instruction has a number, called its *line number*. Here the line numbers are 10 and 20. Normally the machine carries out the commands in numerical order of line numbers—so here it will do line 10 first, line 20 second.

BUT: some commands have the effect of changing the next line number to be carried out. Here the command:

GOTO 10

means 'ignore the next line if there is one, and carry out line 10 instead'.

To understand what the program is doing, we need to know one more thing. The semicolon (;) after the PRINT "HELLO!" statement tells the computer that the *next* item to be printed should follow on immediately after the end of the HELLO! If the semicolon is omitted, the machine will print on the next line of screen instead.

So, when RUN is pressed, this is what the machine does.

It looks for the first line:

10   PRINT "HELLO!";

and carries it out, getting the screen display:

HELLO!

Since that command did *not* tell it to change the pattern of line numbers from the usual one, it goes on to the *next* line in numerical order:

20   GOTO 10

Carrying this out, it gets back to line 10 again! So it now prints another HELLO!, giving:

HELLO!HELLO!

and moves on to line 20. But line 20 sends it back to line 10:

HELLO!HELLO!HELLO!

and it keeps on printing HELLO! forever (or at least until something external, the BREAK key or Old Age or the End of the Universe, stops it). After the sixth occasion it runs off the end of the line and wraps round on to the next; and after about 180 turns it hits the bottom line and the *screen starts to scroll up.* In practice this all happens so fast that you can't see anything except flickering versions of HELLO! as the screen rushes past.

To slow it down, add an extra line:

>   15   WAIT 20

(which I'll explain in Chapter 12). Now the pattern in which the printing takes place is clear.

LISTING

If you've typed a program in, you may at some stage want to have it displayed on the screen in a tidy form, to see what it was. (For instance, you may wish to change a line, but have forgotten its number.) To achieve this, type in immediate mode the command:

>   LIST

Try it now: enter CLS first so that the Oric can't cheat by reading the TV screen.

You can add extra lines to a program just by typing them in. Don't worry about the ordering of the line numbers: the Oric will automatically sort the lines into order. If you type in:

>   20   PRINT "NOT IN ORDER"
>
>   10   PRINT "THIS PROGRAM IS"

and then LIST, it will come out as:

>   10   PRINT "THIS PROGRAM IS"
>
>   20   PRINT "NOT IN ORDER"

Similarly you can *change* a line just by entering a new one with the same number, type:

>   20   PRINT "IN ORDER"

and LIST again.

To delete a line altogether, type its number but nothing else (except RETURN, of course). So:

>   20   (plus RETURN)

deletes line 20. (The computer treats it as a program line with no actual command, only a number, and promptly ignores it.)

To list specific lines (which may be necessary for a long program because of scrolling) you use commands like:

>   LIST 50 – 180

which will list lines 50 to 180. See page 17 of the *Manual* for further information.

NEW AND CLS

There are some simple BASIC commands that require hardly any explanation, but are used all the time to clear out garbage and put the computer in the right frame of mind for a new task. The first is one I mentioned earlier:

>   NEW

This clears out any old program listings. You should *always* type NEW (+ RETURN) before starting to key in a new program, otherwise old program lines can interfere with it.

When the screen is full of junk, the easiest way to clear it, and reset the cursor to top left, is to use:

>   CLS

(Clear Screen.) Recall that CTRL/L does this from the keyboard. On some computers, NEW automatically clears the screen, but the Oric lets you NEW while leaving the screen alone.

You can use both of these in programs; CLS is mandatory in any program that produces a nice display. The only effect of NEW is to produce the Wonderful Self-Destructive Program as soon as that program line is executed!

SIMPLE SAMPLES

Here are three short programs for you to type in and RUN. Each is presented as a project, because your job is to find out what they do. Remember to type NEW (+ RETURN) before entering each program.

Project 1

Type this in (don't forget RETURN after each line!) and RUN it. What happens?

```
10   N$ = "MARMADUKE"
20   PRINT
30   PRINT N$
40   N$ = "I'VE PRINTED ("+ N$ + ")"
50   ZAP
60   WAIT 100
70   GOTO 20
```

Project 2

```
10   FOR T = 0 TO 1000
20   PRINT T, "SQUARED IS", T * T
30   NEXT T
```

Project 3

(Use CTRL/C to stop this.)

```
10   CLS
20   R = 26 * RND(1)
30   C = 38 * RND(1)
40   A = 16 + 8 * RND(1)
50   PLOT C, R, A
60   GOTO 20
```

LINE NUMBERS IN BASIC

Not all high-level languages use line numbers to tell the machine in what order to carry out commands; but there is always *some* definite order. However, some instructions are designed to affect this natural order, thereby sending the machine back to repeat an earlier instruction (possibly subject to slight changes). It is this mixture of precise instructions and variable order in which they are performed, that makes the computer so flexible.

In BASIC, and some other languages, every instruction is numbered. On the Oric you can use numbers between 0 and 63999. You do *not* have to number the lines 1, 2, 3, and so on; in fact it is common to start off using something like 10, 20, 30, . . . going up in tens. The object is to *leave space* to add extra lines in between if you later decide you need to: it would be hard to add a line between lines 2 and 3 of a program! But there is no rule that the numbers must be *regular:* you could number the lines 17, 18, 25, 356, 999, 1000, 1003, 1010, 1020, 5033 (say) if you wished. Most programs start with tidy-looking line numbers and end up with messy ones as mistakes are put right.

MULTI-STATEMENT LINES

You can put several commands on one line of program, provided you separate them by colons (:). For example:

```
10   CLS
20   PRINT "HELP! I AM A PRISONER IN AN ORIC!:
     PING: WAIT 50: GOTO 20
```

This can save space, and typing time; but it's not always such a good idea because:

1. You can only jump to the *start* of a multi-statement line.
2. Changing the line if there's a typing error will be harder.

However, there are occasions when using multiple statements like this saves a lot of work and causes no problems. For example, when assigning a whole lot of variables (see Chapter 6):

```
10   A = 1: B = 2: C = 3: D = 4: E = 5
```

In some of my listings you will occasionally find multiple statement lines, so I thought you ought to know about them. But you can manage perfectly well without them, and they certainly should not be used too heavily or the program becomes unreadable. A well-known publisher of educational software *forbids* multi-statement lines for precisely this reason.

THE TASK OF THE PROGRAMMER

It should now be clear what the task of the programmer is. In order to achieve a particular aim, the programmer must assemble a set of instructions which, when carried out *exactly* by the computer, achieves the desired result.

It is important to realize that the computer has no idea what the 'purpose' of a program is. It simply obeys instructions: it is a fast-thinking and utterly pedantic slave, and if you tell it do something stupid, it will. As you will most certainly discover very quickly when you set about writing programs.

ANSWERS

Project 1

First, the computer prints:

MARMADUKE

Then it notices what it's done, and says so:

I'VE PRINTED (MARMADUKE)

Then it notices *that:*

I'VE PRINTED (I'VE PRINTED(MARMADUKE))

and so on until you get an error message:

and stops. This just means that the thing it's trying to print out has got too long for it to handle.

Project 2

This prints out a table of squares. (The *square* of a number is what you get when you multiply it by itself; for instance 6 squared is 6 × 6 (or 6 * 6 in BASIC) which is 36.) The table continues until it reaches:

1000 SQUARED IS 1000000

and then stops.

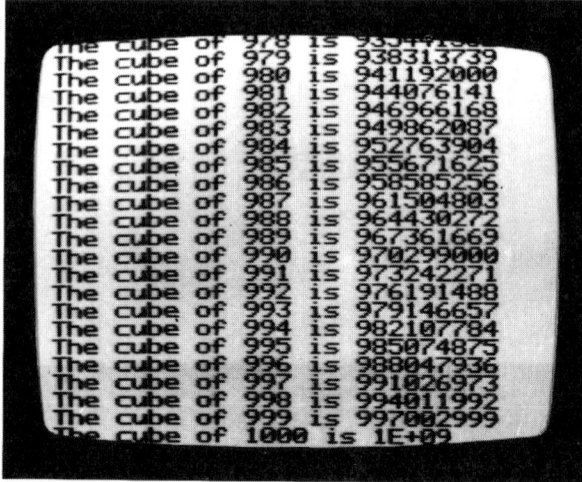

*Figure 4.1   Change T * T to T * T * T and squares to cubes for a variation on Project 2.*

Project 3

This produces a changing pattern of coloured stripes on the screen, running horizontally: it's a foretaste of Oric's colour facilities. Note that each *new* stripe runs from a position somewhere on the screen and continues all the way to the right hand edge; but an old stripe may be overwritten by a new one.

This program will continue indefinitely, until you break using CTRL/C.

The keyboard lets you talk to your Oric. By using the TV screen, it can talk back.

5 Text Display

I've already used the (rather self-explanatory) command:

PRINT

to produce output to the TV screen. The time has come to explore it in more detail.

DISPLAY MODES

The Oric's screen display can work in four different ways, depending on how it's been set up. These *modes,* as they are called, are:

TEXT
LORES0   Low resolution or coarse.
LORES1
HIRES   High resolution or fine.

When you switch the Oric on, it automatically goes into TEXT mode, which gives a blank white screen and lets you plot letters and symbols from the keyboard. For LORES0 and LORES1 see Chapter 19; for HIRES see Chapter 25.

If this idea of several different modes seems a little daunting, think of the machine as having four different notepads, which it uses for different purposes. All you have to do is tell it which notepad to use. Here I'm sticking to TEXT which is automatic anyway unless you tell Oric otherwise.

PRINT

The Oric deals with two different types of information: *numbers* and *strings.* Numbers are displayed in their usual form, possibly with minus signs and decimal points: things like:

25
−999
76.3332

Strings are just a series of symbols, or *characters,* considered as a single entity. To emphasize this, they are normally placed in quotes:

"MARMADUKE"
"CATCH-22"
"*** THE END ***"
"%&4999BCXXX/**GARBAGE+++>"

The PRINT command operates in a very slightly different way, depending on what's being printed.

To PRINT a *number*, such as 42, you just use a program line like:

430   PRINT 42

To print a *string,* you place it within quotes:

440   PRINT "MARMADUKE"

If you try these 'programs' (don't forget RETURN) and RUN them, you'll find that the first gives:

42

on the TV screen, and the second:

MARMADUKE

as you might expect. The difference is that *the quotes round a string are not printed.*

PUNCTUATED PRINTING

A PRINT command can be followed by one of three punctuation marks:

1. Semicolon (;).
2. Comma (,).
3. Nothing at all.

Corresponding examples would be things like:

1. 100 PRINT "THIS MAKES A HUMBLE COMPUTER VERY HAPPY";
2. 110 PRINT "THIS MAKES A HUMBLE COMPUTER VERY HAPPY",
3. 120 PRINT "THIS MAKES A HUMBLE COMPUTER VERY HAPPY"

Consider this as a three-line program, key it in, and RUN: you'll find that the messages start in different positions on the screen.

What the punctuation marks do is *insert spaces* after what's been printed, thereby adjusting the next PRINT position on screen. They affect numbers differently from strings (this is intended for your convenience but personally I'm skeptical), like this:

	Numbers	Strings
Semicolon	Leave one space	Leave no spaces
Comma	Leave four spaces	Leave three spaces
Nothing	Move to next line	Move to next line

While we're at it, let me mention that plain:

PRINT

just prints a blank line and moves on to the next—like CARRIAGE RETURN and LINE FEED on a typewriter. In computer jargon this operation is called a NEWLINE.

The reason for having these punctuation possibilities is that you can produce different *formats* of TV screen output. The main feature is that more than one item may be specified in a single PRINT command, provided punctuation marks are used to *separate* the items. For instance, you could write:

500   PRINT "FRED", "LAURA"; 77, 4.22; "ROGER∇AND∇OUT"

and get a display:

FRED∇∇∇LAURA ∇77∇∇∇∇4.22ROGER∇AND∇OUT

Now that's not terribly pretty; but Project 1 produces neater results.

Project 1

Compare the results of the following 'programs'.

(a)　10　PRINT 1
　　　20　PRINT 2
　　　30　PRINT 3
　　　40　PRINT 4

(b)　10　PRINT 1, 2, 3, 4

(c)　10　PRINT 1; 2; 3; 4

(d)　10　PRINT 1,,2,,3,,4

(e)　10　PRINT 1,,2,,3,,4
　　　20　PRINT 5,,6,,7,,8

(f)　10　PRINT 1,,2,,3,,4,,
　　　20　PRINT 5,,6,,7,,8

(g)　10　PRINT 1,,2,,3,,4
　　　20　PRINT
　　　30　PRINT 5,,6,,7,,8

(h)　Try the programs in (a)-(g) again, but replace 1,2, . . . , 8 by the strings "A", "B", . . . , "H".
(i)　As (h), but now use strings with varying lengths, such as "MARMADUKE", "ORIC", "*", "JR", "CAT", "CABBAGE" and so on.

Take a look at projects 1 and 2 of Chapter 4 and work how the PRINT commands there produce the observed output when the program is run.

Short cut

Instead of typing the word:

　　PRINT

you can use a single question mark:

　　?

This saves memory and typing time at the expense of being less immediately comprehensible. I suggest you get used to PRINT first, then switch to the question mark. For ease of comprehension, I'll always use PRINT in this book. The Oric has plenty of memory to spare anyway!

ANSWERS

Project 1

(a)　1
　　　2
　　　3
　　　4

(b) 1▽▽▽2▽▽▽3▽▽▽4

(c) 1▽2▽3▽4

(d) 1▽▽▽▽▽▽2▽▽▽▽▽▽3▽▽▽▽▽▽4

(e) 1▽▽▽▽▽▽2▽▽▽▽▽▽3▽▽▽▽▽▽4
     5▽▽▽▽▽▽6▽▽▽▽▽▽7▽▽▽▽▽▽8

(f) 1▽▽▽▽▽▽2▽▽▽▽▽▽3▽▽▽▽▽▽4▽▽▽▽▽▽5▽▽▽▽▽
     ▽▽6▽▽▽▽▽▽7▽▽▽▽▽▽8

(g) 1▽▽▽▽▽▽2▽▽▽▽▽▽3▽▽▽▽▽▽4
            (blank line)
     5▽▽▽▽▽▽6▽▽▽▽▽▽7▽▽▽▽▽▽8

(h), (i) As above, but with 1 less space between items.

In many programs, you need to take several numbers, and manipulate them in a particular way; but the numbers themselves may need to change. That's the time to use:

6 Variables

Often a program has to perform the same job on lots of different numbers. For instance, Project 2 in Chapter 4:

    10   FOR T = 0 TO 1000
    20   PRINT T; "SQUARED IS", T * T
    30   NEXT T

This has to work out the square T * T of the number T as it ranges from 0 to 1000. (See Chapter 10 for FOR . . . NEXT.) We say that T is a (numeric) *variable*. As well as having a fixed name, here T, it has a *value* that may change during the course of a program. Here it starts with value 0, then acquires value 1, and so on, until at the end its value is 1000.

Every variable has a *name*. The first character in the name must be a letter, but the others can be any combination of letters and digits. However:

1. There is no limit to the length (except that it has to be less than 78 characters to fit when typed in).
2. The computer only looks at the first *two* characters, so the extra power available from long names is largely illusory.

For example:

    P
    P5
    K
    FRED
    MULLIGATAWNY ▽ SOUP

are valid names, but:

    2K
    *WARS
    $43

are not. And the computer will *not* distinguish between variables named as follows:

FRED	FR	FR7
FREDA	FRANCE	FR12
FREDERICK	FREESPACE	FROGSPAWN

because it will 'think' of all these as being just the two letters FR. However, it is sometimes convenient for the programmer to use longer names, like PRICE or BALANCE or TAX ∇ RATE, as a reminder of what they stand for in the program. The only *danger* is that you may have two variables whose names *look* different, like:

    BALANCE   BACKPAY

but which the computer thinks are the same because they're both BA.

ILLEGAL NAMES

In fact there's one other rule that might cause you some head-scratching if it's not pointed out. If *any part* of a name is one of the BASIC command words, then the word cannot be used for a variable. For instance:

    PRINTRUN

is illegal since it starts PRINT. If you try to use this, the computer gives the error message:

    ?SYNTAX ERROR

It's not just at the start of the word that the trouble occurs. For example, since ON is a BASIC keyword, none of the following are valid variable names:

L<u>ON</u>DON	M<u>ON</u>TY	C<u>ON</u>TENTS	B<u>ON</u>GODRUMS
M<u>ON</u>DAY	FR<u>ON</u>T	MO<u>ON</u>5	B<u>ON</u>E44

You can easily think up some more. (That's why J<u>ON</u>I won't work despite page 21 of the *Manual.*)

10 SPIDER = 8

? SYNTAX ERROR IN LINE 10

I ARREST YOU FOR ASSIGNING AN ILLEGAL VARIABLE

Project 1

Two of the following are valid names, the rest are not. Which, and why? (Hint: ask the Oric to PRINT each one.)

#NINE   BLEND   BATNOSE   JUNCTION   221B   BAKER
STREET   CHESHIRES   MENDACITY   COST   TARGET   IMPOSE
TILLNUMBER   GRANDSIRE   NOTE   WORKRATE   OVERLORD
PREMISE   BARNDANCE

ASSIGNMENT OF A VARIABLE

The computer treats everything that looks like a variable as if it *is* a variable, and it assumes that its value is 0 unless you say otherwise. There are two ways to assign a value to a variable. One is to use the LET command:

    10   LET K = 365

The short way is to omit the word LET! This would give the equally acceptable:

    1Ø   K = 365

The value can be assigned indirectly, by expressing the new variable as some combination of variables already defined. Thus:

    1Ø   LET A = 36
    2Ø   LET B = 5
    3Ø   LET K = 1Ø * A + B

sets K to the value 1Ø * 36 + 5, that is, 365 again. For example, this program will multiply the two numbers 77 and 88:

    1Ø   LET A = 77
    2Ø   LET B = 88
    3Ø   LET K = A * B
    4Ø   PRINT K

And you can change the lines 1Ø and 2Ø to multiply other numbers if you wish. Of course here there are shorter ways to do the same thing, such as:

    1Ø   LET K = 77 * 88
    2Ø   PRINT K

or just:

    1Ø   PRINT 77 * 88

but that's because I've chosen an unusually simple example.

Project 2

At Tangerine Departmental Stores a jewelled tiara costs $135, a magic bull's eye $32 and a packet of lizard-scales $3. Use three variables TIARA, BULL and LIZ to set up a program to calculate the cost of six tiaras, five eyes and twenty-nine packets of lizard-scales. Call this variable PRICE.

Project 3

By changing only one line in the program, calculate the cost of eleven tiaras, fourteen eyes and three packets of lizard-scales.

Project 4

By changing three more lines, answer Project 2 when the prices have changed to $147 for a tiara, $43 for a bull's eye and $1 for a packet of lizard-scales (which are going out of fashion).

STRING VARIABLES

Variables can also be used to hold *string* values: this time the symbol $ (usually pronounced 'string' rather than 'dollar' but you may be feeling mercenary . . .) must be tacked on to the end of the name, like this:

    FRED$ X$ BAKER$ BOW$ G$ MARMADUKE$

Suppose you want to print your name all over the screen. You could write a program like this:

```
10   NAME$ = "MARMADUKE FAUNTLY-SNODE"
20   PRINT NAME$;
30   GOTO 20
```

Here NAME$ is being used as a string variable—but it's not actually varying yet. Now try:

```
10   NAME$ = "MARMADUKE FAUNTLY-SNODE"
20   PRINT NAME$,
30   NAME$ = "MARVIN RUNCID"
40   PRINT NAME$,
50   GOTO 10
```

and see how NAME$ assumes whichever value it has just been assigned. For more on strings, see Chapters 16, 17.

ANSWERS

Project 1

The valid names are BAKER and STREET. The names #NINE and 221B don't start with letters. The rest include a BASIC keyword (or several) as follows: B**LEN**D B**AT**N**OS**E   JUNCTI**ON**   CHES**HI**RES   M**END**ACITY   C**OS**T TAR**GET**   IM**POS**E   TIL**L**NUMBER   GR**AND**SIRE   N**OT**E W**OR**KRATE   OVERL**ORD**   PRE**MIS**E   BAR**ND**ANCE.

Project 2

```
10   CLS
20   TIARA = 135
30   BULL = 32
40   LIZ = 3
50   PRICE = 6 * TIARA + 5 * BULL + 29 * LIZ
60   PRINT "THE TOTAL COST IS $"; PRICE
```

(I've omitted explicit mention of the spaces in the message on line 60: from now on I'll do this if it's clear where they ought to go.)

Project 3

Change line 50 to:

```
50   PRICE = 11 * TIARA + 14 * BULL + 3 * LIZ
```

Project 4

Change lines 20–40 to:

```
20   TIARA = 147
30   BULL = 43
40   LIZ = 1
```

To feed information into the computer,
just instruct it to remind you when
it needs to know something.

7 Inputs

Projects 2–4 of the previous chapter did the job, all right; but it's an awful nuisance having to change program lines every time you want to change the value of a variable. Fortunately this is not necessary, thanks to the command:

INPUT

which lets you set up the value from the keyboard. Like this:

10 PRINT "TYPE IN A NUMBER"

20 INPUT N

30 PRINT "THE NUMBER WAS ▽ "; N

When you run this you'll get TYPE IN A NUMBER and then a question-mark. If you now type a number on the keyboard, and hit RETURN, the program will go on to line 30 and print out its message, plus your number.

MULTIPLE INPUTS

As in PRINT commands, you can INPUT several different variables, using commas to separate them. Try this:

10 INPUT A, B, C

20 PRINT A, B, C

27

You will get a ? sign: key in a number, say 3. Now you get?? for the second number: key in 5. Finally you get ?? again, so key in 7. The Oric promptly prints out the values 3, 5, 7 that you have input for A, B, C; the final result looks like this:

```
RUN
? 3
?? 5
?? 7
3          5          7
Ready
```

PROMPTS

You can print out a message to remind you what an input is *for* (a ? sign is not always helpful), like this:

    10   INPUT "TYPE IN A NUMBER"; N

which has the same effect as lines 10 and 20 of the program that began this chapter. You can use multiple inputs with these *prompt* messages too. Note where the semicolon and the quotes go.

Here's a better way to handle Projects 2–4 of the previous chapter in a general fashion.

```
10   CLS
20   INPUT "PRICES: TIARA, EYE, LIZARD?"; TI, BU, LI
30   INPUT "QUANTITIES?"; NT, NB, NL
40   PRICE = NT * TI + NB * BU + NL * LI
50   PRINT "TOTAL PRICE IS $"; PRICE
```

To keep the listing short I've abbreviated to two-character variables. TI, BU and LI are the old TIARA, BULL, LIZ; and I've got three new variables for the quantities of each, called NT, NB, NL.

GETTING A TIDY DISPLAY

Suppose you want to get someone to enter his age and telephone number, say. Your first attempt might go like this:

```
10   CLS
20   INPUT "AGE"; A
30   PRINT A
40   INPUT "TELEPHONE NUMBER"; T
50   PRINT T
```

It works, but at the end the screen looks like this:

```
AGE? 17
17
TELEPHONE NUMBER? 361005
361005
Ready
```

which isn't exactly pretty. You could do better by changing the order a bit:

```
10   CLS
20   INPUT "AGE?"; A
30   INPUT "TELEPHONE NUMBER?"; T
40   CLS
50   PRINT A, T
```

But sometimes you may not want to wait till the end to print everything out. A better way would then be to arrange for the messages to be printed near the top of the screen, and rub them out before going any further.

At first sight this looks hard to manage, because the *Manual* gives no command to control the position of INPUT prompts on the screen. Indeed the INPUT position seems to have a life of its own. Of course CLS sends the cursor back to top left (and the INPUT prompts appear there too); but it has the unfortunate property of wiping out the entire display, which isn't always what you want.

However, there is a trick. One of the control characters will send the cursor back to top left *without* clearing the screen. The relevant command is:

PRINT CHR$(30)

and I intend to use this for the moment without explaining what CHR$ does, otherwise I'll get sidetracked. It works like this:

```
10   CLS
20   PRINT CHR$(30)
30   INPUT "AGE"; A
40   INPUT "TELEPHONE NUMBER"; T
50   PRINT:PRINT:PRINT
60   PRINT A, T
70   GOTO 20
```

Line 50 is just to separate out the PRINTing of the input values. RUN this, and watch where the input prompts appear: always at the top of screen, even though the last lot of PRINTing remains in view. The program cycles indefinitely, asking for new inputs.

One flaw is that the old input information is also left on screen and gets in the way. Try adding:

```
22   PRINT "   [38 spaces]    "
24   PRINT "   [38 spaces]    "
26   PRINT CHR$(30)
```

This wipes out the old prompts before returning the cursor to top left (in line 26) for the new ones.

You'll still find a few traces of old telephone numbers lying around if you input very long numbers like 999999999999. To get rid of them, modify line 60 to:

60   PRINT A, T;"   [15 spaces or so]   "

Incidentally, when I write things like [38 spaces] what I *mean* is for you to hit the spacebar 38 times:

PRINT "▽▽▽▽▽▽▽▽▽▽▽▽▽▽▽▽▽▽▽▽▽▽▽▽▽▽▽▽▽▽▽▽▽▽
▽▽▽▽▽▽"

If, like me, you're too lazy to want to go through all of that, you can use the command:

22   PRINT SPC(38)

In general SPC(N) produces a string of N spaces, where N is an integer between 0 and 255 inclusive.

DATA, READ, RESTORE

This is a good place to introduce an alternative to INPUT that's useful when you have to set up a standard list of values for certain variables.

The READ statement is rather like INPUT except that instead of picking up data from the keyboard, it gets it from a DATA statement.

Suppose there's a line:

10   READ A

and anywhere else in the program (say at line 250):

250   DATA 37

Then, when line 10 is executed, A will contain 37. Once the '37' has been used, any READ statement executed later will search further on for something to READ so that:

10   READ A
20   READ B

     .
     .
     .

250   DATA 37
260   DATA 15

will set A to 37 and B to 15. You could also write:

10   READ A, B

     .
     .
     .

250   DATA 37, 15

with the same effect. DATA lines can go anywhere: only the order is important.

If you want to re-read the *same* data, it's possible to do this by issuing a RESTORE command. So a line 30:

30   READ X, Y

will transfer 37 to X and 15 to Y provided it's preceded by:

25   RESTORE

See Chapters 22, 28 for examples of these commands in programs.

Sometimes the computer must perform
different tasks under different conditions.
To achieve this, use:

8 Branching

We've met one command that affects the order in which the computer carries out commands, namely GOTO, which sends it to a given line. This is a little *too* regular for programs that have to react differently in different circumstances.

One way to make the program *branch* according to the circumstances is the command:

IF . . . THEN . . .

Here's an example:

BANK BALANCE

This is a very simple example of a 'practical' program. It will work out your bank balance if you tell it your previous balance and list your income and expenditure item by item. To keep it simple I've not worried about the positions of the input messages, but you can think about tidying them up if you wish.

```
 10  CLS
 20  PRINT "PREVIOUS BALANCE IS";
 30  INPUT B
 40  PRINT "LIST DEBITS"
 50  INPUT D
 60  IF D < 0 THEN GOTO 90
 70  LET B = B - D
 80  GOTO 50
 90  PRINT "LIST CREDITS"
100  INPUT D
110  IF D < 0 THEN GOTO 140
120  LET B = B + D
130  GOTO 100
140  PRINT "CURRENT BALANCE IS ▽";B
```

The crucial lines here are 60 and 110. To see how they work, you need to know that the sign '<' means *less than*. So the *condition* $D < 0$ means 'D is less than zero'. This isn't a number, so it doesn't have a numerical value: instead it is a logical statement, and is either *true* or *false* (depending on whether D *is* less than zero, or not). For example:

$3 < 0$ is *false*
$-7 < 0$ is *true*

A typical IF . . . THEN statement will take the form:

IF condition THEN command

If the condition is true, then the command is carried out. But if the condition is false, *the program goes on to the next line.* So line 60, for example sends the program to line 90 if D is negative, but to the next line, line 70, if D is positive.

Now let's see how it works. It should be clear enough up to line 50. Let's suppose you have three debits (outgoings of cash) of 15, 7, and 11 pounds (or dollars if you prefer—at the present rate they'll soon be the same) respectively. On first being asked to input D you tell the computer the first one:

? 15

Since $D < 0$ is *false* it goes on to line 70 and line 80, which *sends it back for another input* at 50. So now you give it the second debit:

? 7

and after that the third:

? 11

but now it's still hungry for an input:

?

so you've got to do something. That's where the $D < 0$ comes in. Input a negative value, the obvious one being −1. Now it goes to line 90, because $D < 0$ is *true*. The whole process repeats now for credits (incoming cash); and the inputs end when you give it −1 again.

The use of a nonsensical input value like −1 to control a branch is a common trick: we say that −1 acts as a *delimiter* because it signals 'end of input list' to the machine.

Meanwhile lines 70 and 120 have deducted debits and added credits, so the final balance is calculated correctly.

Project 1

Write a program to add up the prices in a shopping list, using a delimiter −1 to signal the end of the inputs.

Project 2

Write a program to input a number, and print out whether it is less than 100, equal to 100, or greater than 100. (Hint: > means 'greater than'.)

ORDER RELATIONS ON NUMBERS

There are a whole lot of symbols to decide if one number is larger than another, or the same, or different, or whatever. Here's a complete list, with examples.

$=$	Equal (3 = 3 true; 3 = 4 false).
$>$	Greater than (3 > 2 true; 3 > 4 false).
$<$	Less than (3 < 4 true; 3 < 2 false).
$<>$	Not equal (3 <> 2 true; 3 <> 3 false).
$> =$	Greater than or equal (3 > = 3, 3 > = 2 true; 3 > = 4 false).
$< =$	Less than or equal (3 < = 3, 3 < = 4 true; 3 < = 2 false).

LOGIC

The command words AND and OR can be used to combine conditions. If c and d represent conditions, then c AND d is true provided *both* c and d are. So:

$X > 0$ AND $X < 3$

is true only when X is greater than 0 and also less than 3. For whole numbers X this means X must be 1 or 2; for decimals (which I've not discussed yet) it allows rather more possibilities.

In the same way c OR d is true provided at least one of c and d is (perhaps both). So:

X < 5 OR X = 5

means the same as X < = 5

Finally, I should mention the logical command:

NOT

which changes true to false, and vice versa.

CONDITIONAL JUMPS

One common use of IF . . . THEN is to redirect the program to a new line, like this:

830   IF X = Y THEN GOTO 990

840   whatever . . .

This is called a *conditional jump*. On the Oric it may be shortened to:

830   IF X = Y THEN 990

(that is, the GOTO can be left out).

CONDITIONAL ASSIGNMENTS

Another use is to give a variable different values according to the truth or falsity of a condition:

890   IF X = Y THEN LET K = 77

900   IF X < > Y THEN LET K = 99

which makes K be 77 if X = Y and 99 if not. The LET can as usual be omitted:

890   IF X = Y THEN K = 77

900   IF X < > Y THEN K = 99

Project 3

The Sales Tax levied on an article in Oric Country, Tangerinia depends on its tax code as follows:

Code 1   (Educational)   2%
Code 2   (Children's goods)   5%
Code 3   (Government use)   0%
Code 4   (The rest)   15%

Write a program which accepts as input the code number and prints out the percentage rate of tax.

ELSE

It's a nuisance having to use two IF . . . THENs to set up two actions: one if a condition is true, the other if it is false. Oric BASIC has an extension of IF . . . THEN which is much more efficient in such cases. This is the command:

IF (condition) THEN (action 1) ELSE (action 2)

33

For instance, lines 890–900 on page 33 can be compressed into:

900   IF X = Y THEN K = 77 ELSE K = 99.

Here we have:

Condition	X = Y	(*logical* statement, either true or false)
Action 1	K = 77	(command)
Action 2	K = 99	(command)

If the condition is *true* then action 1 is taken; if it is false, action 2 is taken instead. That is, if X = Y then action 1 sets K = 77; and if X < > Y then action 2 sets K = 99.

Figure 8.1 shows the ways that IF . . . THEN and IF . . . THEN . . . ELSE operate.

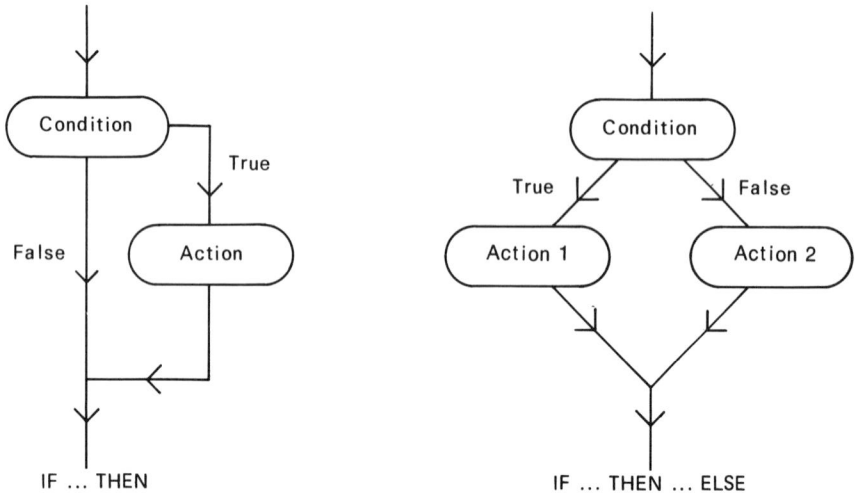

Figure 8.1   Comparison of flow of command in IF . . . THEN and IF . . . THEN . . . ELSE.

ANSWERS

Project 1

```
10   CLS
20   PRINT "SHOPPING LIST"
30   INPUT X
40   IF X < 0 THEN 70
50   SUM = SUM + X
60   GOTO 30
70   PRINT "TOTAL IS ▽"; SUM
```

Project 2

```
10   CLS
20   INPUT N
30   IF N < 100 THEN PRINT "LESS THAN 100"
40   IF N = 100 THEN PRINT "EQUALS 100"
50   IF N > 100 THEN PRINT "GREATER THAN 100"
```

Project 3

```
10  CLS
20  INPUT "TAX CODE?"; TC
30  IF TC < 1 OR TC > 4 THEN 20
40  IF TC = 1 THEN PRINT "2% EDUCATIONAL RATE"
50  IF TC = 2 THEN PRINT "5% CHILDRENS RATE"
60  IF TC = 3 THEN PRINT "0% GOVERNMENT RATE"
70  IF TC = 4 THEN PRINT "15% — TOUGH LUCK MATE!"
```

(Just for fun, I've *mug-trapped* at line 30, that is, protected against nonsensical inputs.)

*The first refinement in communication:
how to control the positioning of the
computer's screen display.*

9 Plot Positions

When in TEXT mode (which is all I've used so far) the TV screen is divided up into 27 rows of *character cells*. Each row is 40 cells long, and each cell can hold one character. The layout is shown in Figure 9.1. The rows are numbered 0–26 and the columns 0–38 as shown. The column in front of column 0 is always reserved by the computer for its own use (it sets the background colour), and in TEXT mode so is column 0 (for the foreground colour). So for now I'll pretend that only columns 1–38 are accessible to us. (*Row* 0 is *not* reserved by the system in any special way.)

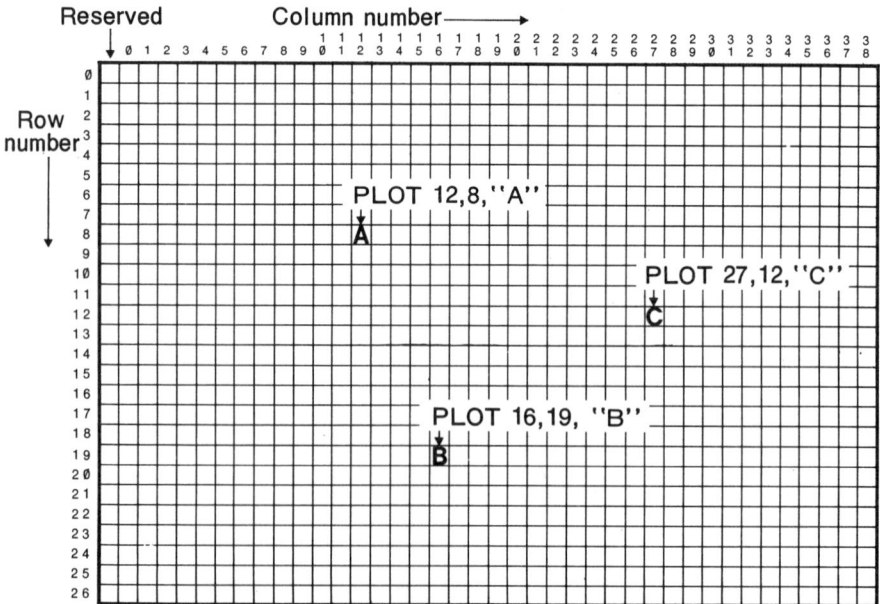

Figure 9.1   TEXT and Low-resolution screen format. Three PLOT positions are marked.

When text is printed to the screen, each character (including spaces) occupies one of these cells. So a program listing:

10   REM TEXT DISPLAY

20   PRINT "ORIC";

30   GOTO 20

is placed on the screen as in Figure 9.2.

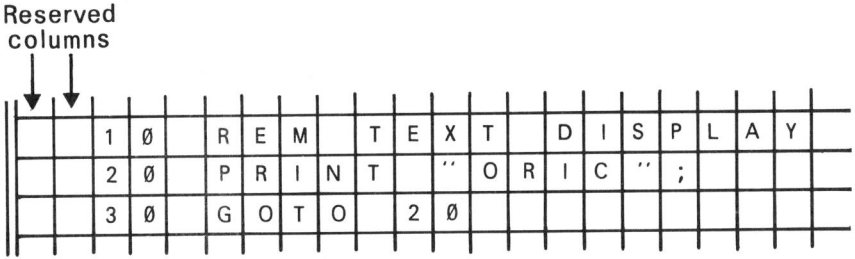

		1	Ø		R	E	M		T	E	X	T		D	I	S	P	L	A	Y	
		2	Ø		P	R	I	N	T		''	O	R	I	C	''	;				
		3	Ø		G	O	T	O		2	Ø										

Figure 9.2   How a program listing is positioned on the Text Screen.

I'm going to call the layout in Figure 9.1 the *Text Screen.* The key to neat displays is the command:

    PLOT C, R, "STRING"

which writes the sequence of characters 'STRING' starting at the cell in column C, row R. (HINT: to remember the order, remind yourself that **C**olumn precedes **R**ow in the alphabet.) For example:

    1Ø CLS

    2Ø PLOT 1Ø, 17, "£"

    3Ø GOTO 3Ø   (to fool the error-message demon)

will plot a £ sign in column 1Ø, row 17. And:

    1Ø CLS

    2Ø PLOT 1Ø, 17, "£1,ØØØ,ØØØ"

    3Ø GOTO 3Ø

will print out £1,ØØØ,ØØØ with the £ sign in the same position.
    Now try this.

    1Ø CLS

    2Ø FOR X = 1 TO 26   (See Chapter 10 for details)

    3Ø PLOT X, X, "£1,ØØØ,ØØØ"

    4Ø NEXT X

    5Ø GOTO 5Ø

Here the million pounds (salute when you say that!) gets printed out in a diagonal line down the screen. That's because, as X goes from 1 to 26, obeying the FOR . . . NEXT instructions (see Chapter 10), the PLOT position goes 1, 1; then 2, 2; then 3, 3 . . . to 26, 26. And those positions run diagonally down the screen as in Figure 9.3.
    If you want to obtain a particular format on the screen, all you have to do is sketch on the Text Screen Grid (Figure 9.1) the positions you want things to be printed in; and then use PLOT with the corresponding entries. For instance, to draw a cross of asterisks in the positions shown in Figure 9.4, you read off from that figure:

    1Ø CLS

    2Ø PLOT 16, 6, "*"

    3Ø PLOT 15, 7, "***"

    4Ø PLOT 16, 8, "*"

    5Ø GOTO 5Ø

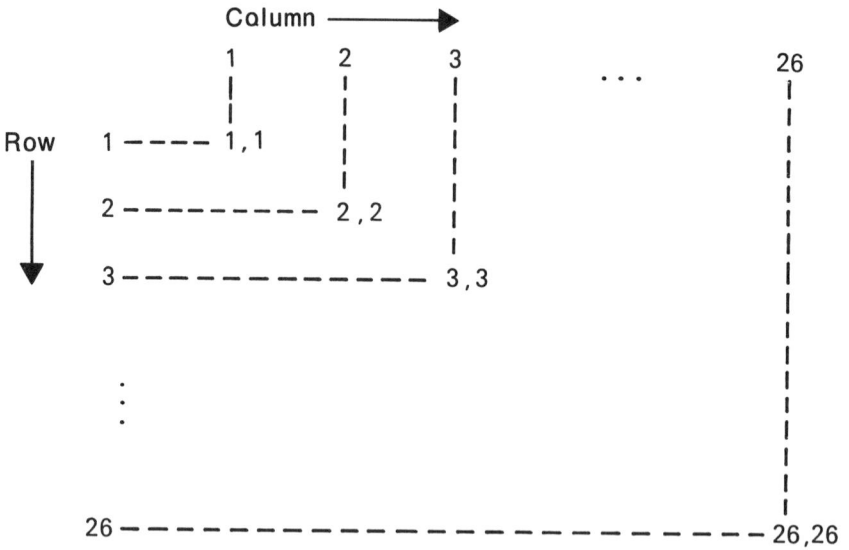

Figure 9.3   PLOT X, X runs diagonally.

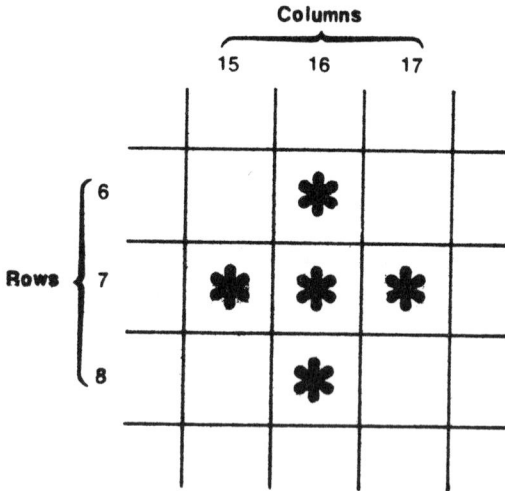

Figure 9.4   Layout for a cross made of asterisks.

Project 1

Print a block of four stars so that its top left corner is in the fifth row and third column, as in Figure 9.5.

Project 2

Choose a position near the middle of the screen and print a square frame of '$' signs like this:

```
$  $  $  $
$        $
$        $
$  $  $  $
```

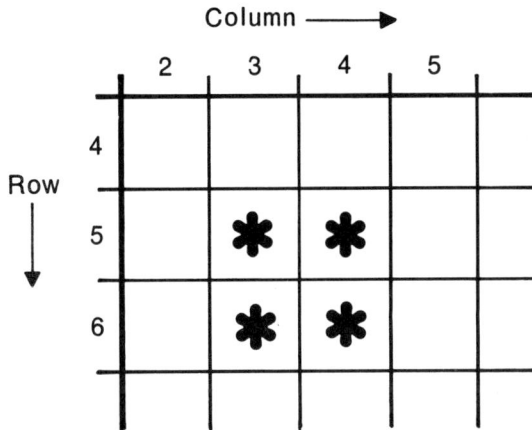

Figure 9.5   Block of four stars for Project 1.

THE MOVING ZIT

We now present a Computer Classic, the basis of many of the early arcade video games, and an excellent introduction to moving graphics and the use of branch commands. Start with this:

```
10  CLS
20  C = 1: R = 3
30  H = 1: V = 1
40  PLOT C, R, "#"
50  C = C + H: R = R + V
60  IF C = 1 OR C = 38 THEN H = −H
70  IF R = 0 OR R = 26 THEN V = −V
80  GOTO 40
```

When you RUN this, a line of '#' signs will grow across the screen at a rapid pace, bouncing off the edges. The bounce effect is produced in lines 60 and 70. The idea is that C, R is the current position of the moving zit #, and H, V are the changes to be made in C and R for the next position (H for horizontal, V for vertical). To begin with H and V are 1, so the zit moves down and to the right; but every time it hits an edge, either H or V reverses direction (see Figure 9.6).

The illusion of motion is fairly strong, but spoilt by the trail of zits left behind. To improve the illusion, we can *erase* each zit once the next has been plotted. First we have to *remember* its position:

```
45  C0 = C: R0 = R
```

Then, when C and R change in line 50, C0 and R0 do not. Having plotted the new zit in line 40, we erase the old one somewhere: a good place (delay the erasure as long as possible to give a less flickering picture) is at line 75:

```
75  PLOT C0, R0, "∇"
```

Away she goes!

Instead of a single zit, let's have a worm, made up of four zits in a row. You can achieve this by putting in a sort of 'delay line' where the PLOT position for erasure is passed down the line one stage each time, until finally it gets acted upon. Delete line 45 above; and replace it by:

```
42  CØ = C1:RØ = R1
44  C1 = C2:R1 = R2
46  C2 = C3:R2 = R3
48  C3 = C:R3 = R
```

If you can work out how the delays do their job, you'll have no trouble at all with:

Project 3

Replace lines 42–48 by seven lines that produce a 7-zit worm.

You haven't heard the last of PLOT, by any means: it can produce colour too! See Chapters 12, 19.

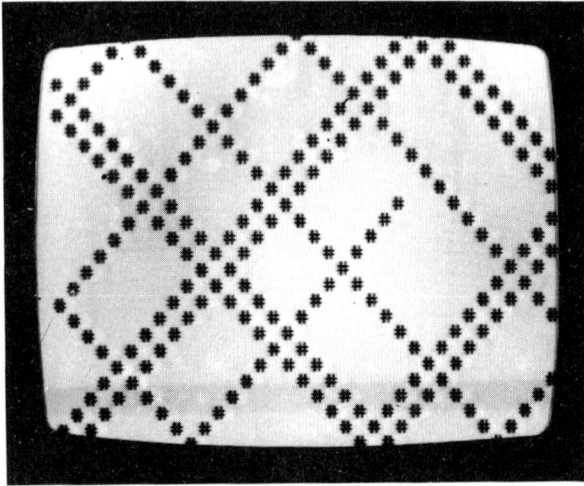

Figure 9.6   First stage of the Moving Zit.

ANSWERS

Project 1

```
10  CLS
20  PLOT 3, 5, "**"
30  PLOT 3, 6, "**"
40  GOTO 40
```

Project 2

```
10  CLS
20  PLOT 18, 11, "$$$$"
30  PLOT 18, 12, "$▽▽$"
```

```
40   PLOT 18, 13, "$▽▽$"
50   PLOT 18, 14, "$$$$"
60   GOTO 50
```

Project 3

Delete lines 42–48 and add:

```
41   C0 = C1:R0 = R1
42   C1 = C2:R1 = R2
43   C2 = C3:R2 = R3
44   C3 = C4:R3 = R4
45   C4 = C5:R4 = R5
46   C5 = C6:R5 = R6
47   C6 = C:R6 = R
```

Obviously there ought to be a neater way to achieve this, by making the computer do all the work. See Chapter 21 on Arrays.

*A fundamental programming technique gets
the computer to carry out a given task
over and over again. Better still, it
can make regular changes to the task as
well. Examples include multiplication
tables and displaying rectangles.*

10 Looping

In this chapter I say more about the FOR . . . NEXT command (used in Project 2 Chapter 4) which tells the machine to perform a given task several times over. This wouldn't be very exciting, if the task were absolutely fixed; but it is possible to make some of the details of the task change at each step. The result is a very powerful addition to the programmer's elbow. I also discuss an alternative, REPEAT . . . UNTIL.

Feeling in an educational mood, I suggest you try out the following program. I'll explain it after you've done so.

MULTIPLICATION TABLES

```
10  CLS
20  PRINT "SEVEN TIMES TABLE"
30  PRINT
40  FOR N = 1 TO 12
50  PRINT N; "X∇7∇ = ∇"; 7 * N
60  NEXT N
```

RUN this: if you haven't made any mistakes, pretty quickly you should get:

```
1 X 7 = 7
2 X 7 = 14
3 X 7 = 21
4 X 7 = 28
5 X 7 = 35
6 X 7 = 42
7 X 7 = 49
8 X 7 = 56
9 X 7 = 63
10 X 7 = 70
11 X 7 = 77
12 X 7 = 84
```

HOW THE LOOP WORKS

This technique is known as a *loop*. The loop starts with the FOR command in line 40, and ends with the NEXT command in line 60. As well as this, we have to set up a number N to act as a *counter*, and tell the machine where to start counting (1) and stop (12). All this is done in line 40:

FOR	(start loop here)
N	(use N as counter)
= 1	(start value for N)
TO	(carry on as far as)
12	(finish value for N)

What happens is this. When the computer first encounters the loop it sets N equal to the start value (1) and carries out the commands until it hits NEXT. It then compares N with the finish value (12) and if N is less than this it increases N by 1 (to get 2) and goes back to the start of the loop, doing the commands all over again. On next meeting NEXT it compares again, and increases N to 3; then to 4, 5, 6, . . . until N becomes 12. When it hits NEXT and finds that now N has reached the finish value of 12, it leaves the loop and carries on to the next program line (if there is one) or stops (if not).

I'll go through this in detail in a second, but first a word about line 50. This is just a series of PRINT commands strung together, and it produces displays like:

1 X 7 = 7

Its spaces ∇ are just to make the result look pretty. This particular display comes when it has the counter N set to value 1, and it arises like this:

PRINT N	PRINT 1	1
;	don't move on	
"X ∇ 7 ∇ = ∇"	PRINT "X ∇ 7 ∇ = ∇"	1 X 7 =
;	don't move on	
7 * N	PRINT 7 * 1 (which is 7)	1 X 7 = 7
(no semicolon)	move on to next line	

Note the use of PRINT N *without* quotation marks. If you write PRINT "N" then it just prints out the single *letter* N. If the quotes are left out, it prints out the *numerical value* assigned to N. Since N starts at 1 and increases step by step to 12, the PRINT N command has the effect of printing the numbers 1, 2, 3, . . . , 12, depending on the stage in the loop.

Similarly 7 * N takes the values 7 * 1 = 1, 7 * 2 = 14, . . . , 7 * 12 = 84; so these numbers are printed in turn too.

Now we can run through the program in sequence and see how it achieves its result.

10	CLS	Clear the screen.
20	PRINT "SEVEN TIMES TABLE"	SEVEN TIMES TABLE
30	PRINT	Print a blank line to leave a space below the heading.
40	FOR N = 1 TO 12	Set up loop with N as counter and ranging from 1 (start) to 12 (finish).
50	PRINT N; "X ∇ 7 ∇ = ∇"; 7 * N	1 X 7 = 7
60	NEXT N	Is N = 12? No, it's 1. Add 1 to N to get 2, and go back to line 50.

5Ø	PRINT N; "X ∇ 7 ∇ = ∇"; 7 * N	2 X 7 = 14
6Ø	NEXT N	Is N = 12? No, it's 2. Bump it up to 3 and go back to 5Ø. Continue this process . . .
6Ø	NEXT N	N is now 12, so exit the loop. There are no more commands: STOP!

Project 1

Change lines 2Ø and 5Ø so that the computer prints out:

1. A five times table;
2. A nine times table;
3. And for the ambitious, a ninety-nine times table.

(Hint: change those 7s to 5, 6 or 99.)

LOOPING PRINT STATEMENTS

By combining loops with PLOT commands, a variety of effects can be obtained. For example, suppose we want to draw a vertical line of nine stars, starting from row 2 of column 5 and going downwards. Then all we need do is:

```
10  CLS
20  FOR R = 2 TO 10
30  PLOT R, 5, "*"
40  NEXT R
50  GOTO 50
```

Here we use the row number R as a counter and print everything in column 5.
    Using a fixed row and a variable column gives a horizontal line:

```
10  CLS
20  FOR C = 2 TO 10
30  PLOT 5, C, "*"
40  NEXT C
50  GOTO 50
```

Changing both row and column will give a diagonal line:

```
10  CLS
20  FOR K = 1 TO 13
30  PLOT K, K, "*"
40  NEXT K
50  GOTO 50
```

Project 2

Combine the techniques for drawing horizontal and vertical lines to put a frame of stars round the outside of the screen but placed one space in from the edge (thus leaving a blank frame round the very outside).

LOOPING THE LOOP

By placing loops inside other loops, more complex effects can be achieved. Suppose we want to draw a rectangle, seven spaces wide and five spaces high, made up of '$' signs. For definiteness let's put the top corner in row 3, column 4.

Each row of the rectangle is a line of characters, which we can draw using a loop as above. Then we need to draw a series of such lines to get the whole rectangle; so we use *another* loop.

Let's build it up slowly. To draw a horizontal line of length 7 in row R, starting at column 4 (and so ending up at column 10) we would use:

```
100   FOR C = 4 TO 10
110   PLOT R, C, "$";
120   NEXT C
```

You could use FOR C = 1 TO 7; but then line 110 has to be PLOT R, C + 3, "$"). Then to draw several lines, with R running from 3 to 7 (for a height of five) we'd need something like this:

```
 50   FOR R = 3 TO 7
      (draw line in row R)
150   NEXT R
```

Now we know what commands will do the 'draw line in row R': they are lines 100–120 above. (I've chosen line numbers so that everything fits together at the end.) So the guts of the program will be this:

```
 50   FOR R = 3 TO 7
100   FOR C = 4 TO 10            inner    outer
110   PLOT R, C, "$"             loop     loop
120   NEXT C
150   NEXT R
```

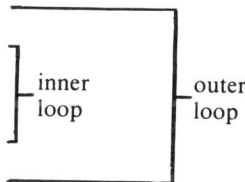

That's essentially it, although to keep it tidy you should do the usual:

```
 10   CLS
200   GOTO 200
```

O-134

SOME DAY YOUR
PRINTs
WILL COME

45

Notice that the line numbers aren't especially tidy; no matter, the Oric doesn't care.

Observe that the way we built this up leads to the whole of the inner loop being between the ends of the outer one. That is, the FORs and NEXTs end up in the order:

FOR C

FOR R

. . .   inner loop   outer loop

NEXT R

NEXT C

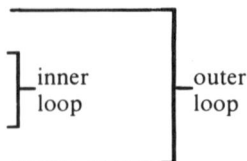

This is important, and the computer will not do what you expect if you get the last two in the wrong order.

Project 3

Overlap two rectangles to draw a cross of Hs shaped like this:

```
        H  H
        H  H
  H  H  H  H  H  H
  H  H  H  H  H  H
        H  H
        H  H
```

STEP SIZE

When you write a command like:

FOR R = 3 TO 14

The Oric *assumes* that it should count up in ones:

3, 4, 5, 6, 7, 8, 9, 10, 11, 12, 13, 14.

But you can change this size by using the command STEP. To count up in twos you would type:

FOR R = 3 TO 14 STEP 2

and it would give R the values:

3, 5, 7, 9, 11, 13

in turn. (It stops there, because the next, 15, would be bigger than the limiting value 14 in the command. It does *not* set R equal to the value 14 at all. However, if you'd written:

FOR R = 3 TO 15 STEP 2

it would give R the values:

3, 5, 7, 9, 11, 13, 15

and the top value 15 in the FOR command *would be reached.*)

Project 4

Change line 40 of the SEVEN TIMES TABLE program so that it only prints out multiples of *even* numbers by 7.

Project 5

Like Project 4, but just the *odd* numbers.

You can even count backwards by using a *negative* step size:

```
10   CLS
20   FOR I = 10 TO 0 STEP −1
30   PRINT I
40   NEXT I
50   PRINT "WE HAVE LIFT-OFF!"
```

Short cut In any NEXT command, the loop counter can be *omitted*. That is, you can write just NEXT instead of NEXT I or NEXT R or whatever. This saves space, but you may lose track of which NEXT is which. (The computer, however, will not!)

REPEAT UNTIL

There is a different way to produce a loop, which is often clearer. It applies especially to cases where the number of times round the loop may depend on things that happen inside the loop.

Here's a game you can play against a friend on the computer. You take it in turns to input 'a number between 1 and 5: the first person to take the total over 99 *loses*.

There are two loops involved. One checks the input to make sure it's between 1 and 5, and if not, asks for it again. The other adds the input to the total, and checks if that's over 99. If so, the program stops.

You can't really do this kind of thing with FOR . . . NEXT: you don't know how long the loops will go on for. The best you could do is something like this:

```
10   SUM = 0 (why can't I use TOTAL?)
20   FOR T = 1 TO 100
30   INPUT D                                    ⎤ inner
40   IF D < 1 OR D > 5 THEN 30                  ⎦ loop     ⎤
50   SUM = SUM + D                                          ⎬ outer loop
60   IF SUM < = 99 THEN 20                                 ⎦
70   NEXT T
80   PRINT "YOU LOSE"
```

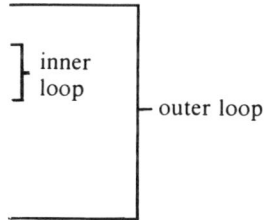

But it's bad practice to jump out of a FOR . . . NEXT loop using (a tacit) GOTO as in line 60. It leaves unwanted junk lying around inside the computer's memory. And we only get away with it at all because we know that the loop is *bound* to terminate in at most 100 cycles. The other 'loop' in lines 30 and 40 might go on forever, so there's no way to use FOR . . . NEXT: instead we use (a silent) GOTO in line 40.

More proper, but far from satisfactory, is a method using only GOTOs:

```
10   SUM = 0
20   INPUT D                                    ⎤ inner
30   IF D < 1 OR D > 5 THEN 20                  ⎦ loop     ⎤
40   SUM = SUM + D                                          ⎬ outer loop
50   IF SUM < = 99 THEN 20                                 ⎦
60   PRINT "YOU LOSE"
```

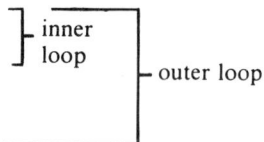

It's easy to get lost among the (yet again silent) GOTOs in lines 30 and 50. In fact GOTOs are somewhat frowned upon in polite (i.e. 'Structured Programming') society, because of this. (Actually, GOTOs *can* be used in a civilized way, so it's best not to get too snobbish about them.)

With REPEAT . . . UNTIL, all is sweetness and light:

```
10   SUM = 0
20   REPEAT
30   REPEAT
40   INPUT D
50   UNTIL D > = 1 AND D < = 5
60   SUM = SUM + D
70   UNTIL SUM > 99
80   PRINT "YOU LOSE"
```

inner loop (lines 30–50) — outer loop (lines 20–70)

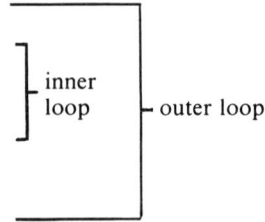

Note the format:

REPEAT

(series of program lines defining the action to be repeated)

UNTIL (condition)

which ensures that the action so defined is repeated until the stated condition is *true*.

Figure 10.1 shows in diagrammatic form the essential structures of FOR . . . NEXT and REPEAT . . . UNTIL loops.

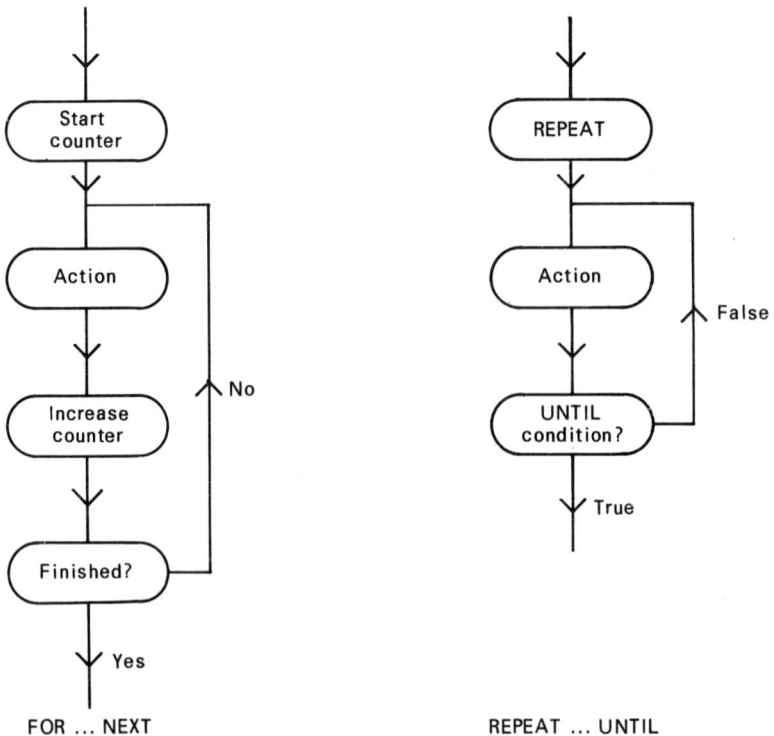

Figure 10.1   Comparison of flow of commands in FOR . . . NEXT and REPEAT . . . UNTIL loops.

ANSWERS

Project 1

1. 20 PRINT "FIVE TIMES TABLE"
   50 PRINT N; "X ▽ 5 ▽ = ▽"; 5 * N

2. 20 PRINT "NINE TIMES TABLE"
   50 PRINT N; "X ▽ 9 ▽ = ▽"; 9 * N

3. 20 PRINT "NINETY-NINE TIMES TABLE"
   50 PRINT N; "X ▽ 99 ▽ = ▽"; 99 * N

Project 2

```
10   CLS
20   FOR C = 1 TO 37      ⎤
30   PLOT C, 1, "*"       ⎬ top line
40   NEXT C               ⎦
50   FOR C = 1 TO 37      ⎤
60   PLOT C, 25, "*"      ⎬ bottom line
70   NEXT C               ⎦
80   FOR R = 2 TO 24      ⎤
90   PLOT 1, R, "*"       ⎬ left side
100  NEXT R               ⎦
110  FOR R = 2 TO 24      ⎤
120  PLOT 37, R, "*"      ⎬ right side
130  NEXT R               ⎦
140  GOTO 140
```

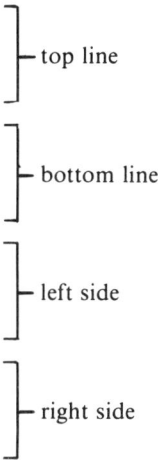

Project 3

```
10   CLS
20   FOR R = 3 TO 8       ⎤
30   FOR C = 20 TO 21     ⎥
40   PLOT R, C, "H"       ⎬ first rectangle
50   NEXT C               ⎥
60   NEXT R               ⎦
```

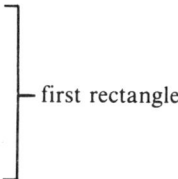

```
 70   FOR R = 5 TO 6            ⎤
 80   FOR C = 18 TO 23          │
 90   PLOT R, C, "H"            ⎬— second rectangle
100   NEXT C                    │
110   NEXT R                    ⎦
120   GOTO 120
```

Project 4

```
 40   FOR N = 2 TO 12 STEP 2
```

Project 5

```
 40   FOR N = 1 TO 11 STEP 2
```

or

```
 40   FOR N = 1 TO 12 STEP 2
```

(Either line works. Don't forget to include all the other lines as before, though!)

It is said that the colourful term 'getting the bugs out' arose in the early days of computing, when insects used to crawl inside the machine and cause short circuits. Nowadays, if the computer goes wrong, it's usually the programmer's fault. But to put it right, you still need to know about . . .

11 Debugging 11

You should never be discouraged when a program doesn't work correctly the first time you run it. Even for professional programmers, it hardly ever does!

So it's important to have at your command techniques which will help you find the errors in a program quickly and easily. That's what we call *debugging*.

SYNTAX ERRORS

To start with, let's examine the kinds of errors which will come to light first when you run a program. For instance, suppose somewhere in a program you write:

    50   FOR N = 1 − 7

forgetting that you have to use 'TO' to separate the values in a FOR loop. Now the Oric will be happy to accept this when you type it in, but when the program is run, you'll get the message:

    ?SYNTAX ERROR IN 50

In other words, the Oric doesn't like the grammatical construction of the statement in line 50. It's rather as if I said "Oric, him not understand this statement". You'd object to my syntax! The only difference is that *you* can make sense of my ungrammatical offering, but the Oric won't *try* to make sense of line 50. It will simply throw it out, as we've seen.

Particularly when you're learning a computer language, you're likely to make quite a few errors of this kind, and it's very annoying to type in a sixty-line program containing ten FOR statements, only to be told when you run it that you've remembered the construction of a FOR statement wrongly, and you'll have to alter all of them. So you should make a habit of typing RUN after every couple of lines you enter. Of course, uncompleted programs probably won't behave sensibly, and you may even get error messages which will go away when the next bit has been typed in, but at this stage you're only interested in finding the syntax errors before you've perpetrated too many of them.

CHOPPING AND CHANGING

Having identified the error, you need to alter the statement. Of course you can always delete a whole line by just typing the line number, followed by RETURN, and you can replace one completely by just typing the new line. However, to do all editing this way would be pretty tedious, particularly if there are quite a few longish lines to be hacked about.

The Oric provides you with a powerful tool which can be used for editing program lines, among (as we shall see) other things. To use it effectively, you must understand clearly the way in which data is transferred from the keyboard to the Oric's memory. See Figure 11.2.

When a key is hit, the symbol on it is transferred to a special chunk of memory called the *input buffer,* and, at the same time, it is displayed on the screen. It does *not*, at this stage, get passed on to the Oric's main memory. That only happens when a whole line has been assembled in the buffer. And how does the system know when this has happened? Because you hit RETURN to tell it!

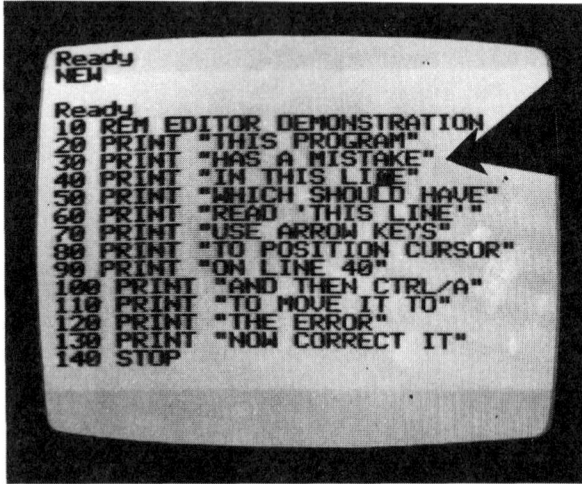

Figure 11.1   Positioning the cursor using CTRL/A during an edit.

So the input buffer is filled until the Oric sees a RETURN from the keyboard. Then, the whole buffer contents are shovelled to main memory and stored or acted upon—depending on whether the symbols passed on represent a program line or a command (or, come to that, data).

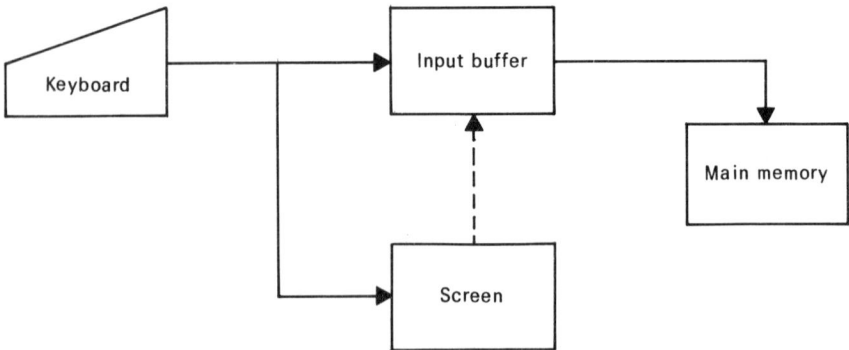

Figure 11.2   Keyboard to memory data transfer.

The eagle-eyed will have noticed that there seems to be another way of getting data into the input buffer—from the screen! (See the dotted line in Figure 11.2). This is indeed possible—all you have to do is hit CTRL/A (hold the CTRL key down and hit A at the same time) and a character will be copied from the screen to the input buffer. But which one? Well, it would make sense to make use of the cursor, and that's exactly what happens; it's the symbol at the current cursor position that is copied to the buffer. CTRL/A has a second effect, which is to move the cursor one character position right.

ADDING TO THE END OF A LINE

Now let's make use of this information. We'll start by adding a REM to an existing line; so that we might have:

230 IF B > 6 THEN PRINT "No Good"

and want to clarify things with:

230 IF B > 6 THEN PRINT "No Good":REM B RANGE IS 1–6

First, make sure that line 230 (original version) is somewhere on the screen. If it isn't type CTRL/L (to clear the screen) and then LIST 230. Now use the cursor keys to position the cursor over the '2'. Use CTRL/A repeatedly to transfer the characters in the line to the input buffer until the cursor is one position after the closing quote marks. Now type in:

:REM B RANGE IS 1–6

and hit RETURN.

What you've done is to *combine* characters coming from the screen with characters coming from the keyboard, in the input buffer. You can do this in numerous ways and nothing will be transferred into main memory until you hit RETURN. Here are some other examples.

CHANGING A LINE NUMBER

You've got the line:

115 IF A < 7 OR B > 10 THEN X = X * X:P = P + 1

and you realize it should be line 1150 instead. Correct it like this:

Type 1150 (but *don't* hit RETURN). Now position the cursor over the 'I' of 'IF'. Use CTRL/A to move the rest of the line into the buffer, where it will join the 1150 already there. Finally, when the cursor is past the '1' at the end of the line, hit RETURN.

It's always worth checking that an edit has done what you intended by typing CTRL/L and then LIST. Do so now. Line 1150 is there all right but, of course, you haven't overwritten line 115 so that's still there too! There are occasions when you want identical, or at least, very similar lines in a program, and this is a useful technique then, but in this example you would have to get rid of line 115 by typing 115 and then RETURN.

DELETING PART OF A LINE

Suppose you have an initialization line:

10 P = 1:N = 20:R = 0:Z = 0:M = 0:A = 4

and during the program's development, you realize that N and R do not need to be set up at this stage, so you'd like the line to read:

10 P = 1:Z = 0:M = 0:A = 4

Position the cursor at the beginning of the line, as usual. Transfer:

10 P = 1:

to the buffer using CTRL/A. Now use the cursor right (→) key to skip over:

N = 20:R = 0:

When the cursor is over 'Z' use CTRL/A again to transfer the other characters to the buffer, and finally hit RETURN.

ALTERING CHARACTERS

The line:

240 IF A = 4 THEN FRED = 20

should read:

240   IF A = 4 THEN BERT = 20

(No, I don't know why, either! Maybe because FRED is illegal—why?)

Set the cursor to the beginning of the line and transfer characters to the input buffer using CTRL/A until the cursor is over 'F'. Type 'BERT'. These letters will, of course, be transferred to the input buffer, but, because of the cursor position, you will also see them overwrite 'FRED' on the screen. (This is, to all intents and purposes, coincidental, and it is important not to think about the editing process as taking place on the screen, even though, in this one case, it looks like it.) The cursor is now over '=' so three more CTRL/As will transfer the '= 20', and then you can hit RETURN.

ADDING CHARACTERS WITHIN A LINE

Suppose that our line 240 above is to be altered from FRED to BERTRAM instead of just BERT (again, for reasons of less than total clarity).

Now, with the experience of the last example behind you, it should be apparent that there's a nasty problem here, because if you proceed as before, the 'RAM' will overwrite '= 20' on the screen so that these characters are no longer available to be transferred to the buffer. Of course, you could retype '= 20' but this could be a real nuisance if the line were longer.

You can deal with the problem like this. Go as far as inserting 'BERT' as before, so the cursor is now over '='. Now move the cursor to *another line*. It doesn't matter where, as long as it's no longer interfering with the line you're trying to edit. Usually, a convenient spot is one line up. Type 'RAM'. This will, of course, appear in the input buffer. Now use the cursor keys to return to the '=' sign, and transfer the '= 20' using CTRL/A. Finally, hit RETURN, as usual.

You will probably have messed up the screen display during this process by overwriting a chunk of some poor unsuspecting line with the letters 'RAM'. Don't worry; you have done no harm. Never forget that it is only what is in the input buffer that can be transferred to main memory, and as I've said before, you mustn't think of the Oric as having a screen editor—it hasn't.

To convince yourself of this type CTRL/L and LIST.

ORIC'S DATA PARTY TRICK

At the beginning of this chapter, I remarked that the 'copy screen to buffer' feature provided by CTRL/A had uses outside editing. Here's one.

You've written a program which inputs some numbers and does something with them (it doesn't matter what) like this:

```
10   INPUT A
20   IF A = 0 THEN PRINT P:END
...          (processing)
100  GOTO 10
```

Now you want to test it, so you type something like:

```
RUN
? 7.38
? 12.46
? 8.1012
? 21.604
? 0
```

(Of course, it's the Oric which generates the question marks). Anyway, the wrong answer is displayed, and you realize it's because you forgot to take out line 93 as you'd intended (or whatever). So you've got to do the edit, rerun, and type in all the data again.

Or have you? Provided the data is still on the screen, you can use CTRL/A to copy it to the buffer, and when you hit RETURN, the Oric accepts it, neither knowing nor caring that the data came from the screen rather than the keyboard! So you can use the cursor keys to place the cursor over the 'R' of 'RUN', hit CTRL/A 3 times followed by RETURN (see, you don't even have to type RUN) after which the Oric will generate a question mark which will overwrite the first one already on the screen, and move the cursor over the 7. Hit CTRL/A 4 times and 7.38 goes to the buffer. Hit RETURN and it's passed to main memory. The Oric will generate the next question mark, leaving the cursor over the '1' of '12.46' and so on and so on.

Pretty sneaky eh?

Like the early days of the cinema, the simplest computer programs are silent black-and-white productions. But with a few extra commands you can add:

12 Sound and Colour

Deep in the caverns of Pluto, hordes of little green and purple monsters are stealthily sneaking up on you: graunch, graunch, graunch . . .

Yes, well. At the moment they will have to be little *black* monsters, preferably bearing a remarkable resemblance to an Oric keyboard character; and so stealthy will be the sneaking that you won't hear a thing. We can improve the attractiveness of our programs tremendously by adding colour, sound and some interesting graphics. In this chapter I'm only going to do the easy stuff, and I don't apologise for that: the first thing is to get used to handling sound and colour without having to think too hard about fine details. Later chapters (19, 22, 26) carry the story several stages further; but I have to stop somewhere because this book just isn't big enough to hold everything I'd like to tell you.

SOUND

The Oric has a special chip dedicated to the production of sound effects. Four of these are accessible from BASIC using the commands:

EXPLODE

PING

SHOOT

ZAP

which are fairly self-explanatory. Try them as direct commands: now apologise to the cat and help it down off the curtain-rail.

There's one point to take care of when using these commands. To appreciate the difficulty, take a look at this program and decide what the result ought to sound like.

```
10   EXPLODE
20   PING
30   SHOOT
40   ZAP
50   PRINT "FINISHED!"
```

Well, it *ought* to string the four sounds together, one after the other. Try it out and listen.

That's quite odd, isn't it? It's as if each sound effect except the last ZAP is being snuffed out before it has a chance to get going. And that's exactly what's happening. Whenever you ask for a sound effect the sound chip stops whatever it's currently doing and starts doing what you've asked for, even though it may not have finished the *previous* sound effect.

56

The command to get round this problem is:

WAIT

which should be followed by a number telling the computer how long to wait for. (I've used it occasionally already, without explanation, to delay the operation of the machine so that you can observe things that would otherwise change too rapidly.) The number N in:

WAIT(N)

produces a pause of N *hundredths* of a second. So:

WAIT 100

gives a 1-second pause,

WAIT 200

gives a 2-second pause, and so on.

Add the following pauses to the sound effects program:

    15   WAIT 100
    25   WAIT 100
    35   WAIT 30
    45   WAIT 30

and you'll be able to hear all four sounds. The WAIT times are about the shortest that will work satisfactorily, but you can experiment if you think you can do better. So:

    EXPLODE and PING need a WAIT 100 (about 1 second)
    SHOOT and ZAP need a WAIT 30 (about 0.3 seconds)

if any other sounds are going to follow them. However, commands that don't ask for sounds do not interfere with the sound chip, so you can often omit the WAITs. For more on sound, see Chapter 22.

COLOUR

You've seen a few examples of Oric colour, but not in a systematic way. Full control of the colour system takes a fair amount of practice so I'll start with the simplest ideas and work up.

In TEXT (or LORES) mode, each character cell on the screen is assigned two colours, the *background* and the *foreground*. Sensibly, the commands that affect these (for the *whole* screen) are:

PAPER

INK

These must be followed by a number between 0 and 7, corresponding to the following colours:

Number	Colour
0	Black
1	Red
2	Green
3	Yellow
4	Blue
5	Magenta (purple)
6	Cyan (light blue)
7	White

So the commands:

    PAPER 4

    INK 3

will produce yellow text (INK colour 3 = yellow) on a blue (PAPER colour 4) background. Try them as direct commands; then type things on the screen to see the effect.
Leave the screen uncleared, and type in:

    PAPER 2

    INK 0

You'll find that the colours change over the whole screen, but the text is otherwise unaffected.

Project 1

Write a program to display all eight colours, one after the other, as the PAPER colour on a clear screen—for long enough to be able to see the colours—say two seconds each.

You can use INK and PAPER commands in a program: every time you change the colours, they will change across the entire screen. NEW does *not* reset them to black-on-white, but RESET does.

DIFFERENT COLOURS ON THE SAME SCREEN

That's fun, but not very impressive. It would be more interesting to 'paint' regions of the screen in *different* colours. And in fact this can be done, using what the *Manual* rather offputtingly calls *serial attributes*. Let's take it one step at a time.
The main idea is that the PLOT command can be used to define *colours* as well as *characters* at a given position. Experiment with this:

    10 REPEAT
    20 INPUT T
    30 UNTIL T > = 0 AND T < = 7
    40 PLOT 10, 12, T + 16
    50 GOTO 10

This has a mug-trapped input for a number between 0 and 7. Try each input in turn: what do you notice?
Suppose for instance that T is 2 (the colour code for green). Then *the whole of row 12, from column 10 onwards,* turns green. I'll explain the T + 16 in line 40 in the next section.
What's happening is this. A command like:

    PLOT 10, 12, "X"

produces a character X on the Text Screen. But a command:

    PLOT 10, 12, 18

produces a *colour*—the exact colour depending on the number (here 18) in a way I'll explain later. The colour applies not only to the cell at 10, 12; it also affects the rest of that row. That's what the word *serial* refers to. (The word *attribute* is explained in the next section, page 61.)
The colour change can, of course, be 'turned off' by another PLOT later in the same row. Try this:

PLOT 10, 12, 18

PLOT 20, 12, 21

Now you've got a stripe that starts green and turns magenta.

Basically, that's all you need to know, because careful selection of the PLOT points lets you set up any combination of colours you want. But there are two things to notice:

1. In TEXT mode, the paper colour for a row is set up in the reserved column to the left of column 0. This is *not* accessible by the PLOT command. (It *is* accessible by a more subtle command POKE, but that's a different kettle of fish entirely and I shouldn't have mentioned it.)
2. You cannot PLOT a character *and* a colour to the same character cell. If you PLOT a character to a cell that contains a colour, you wipe out that colour command.

The next program may make this clearer.

```
 10   CLS
 20   COL = 0
 30   FOR C = 0 TO 36 STEP 4
 40   FOR R = 0 TO 26
 50   COL = COL + 1
 60   IF COL > 7 THEN COL = 0
 70   PLOT C, R, COL + 16
 80   NEXT R
 90   NEXT C
100   WAIT 300
110   FOR X = 0 TO 26
120   PLOT X + 1, X, "WHAMMO!"
130   WAIT 50
140   NEXT X
```

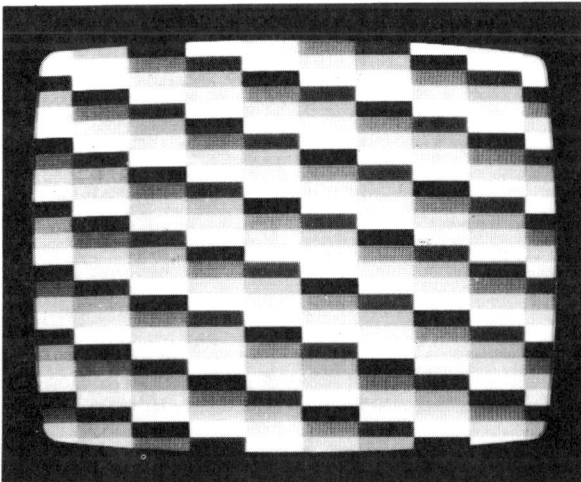

Figure 12.1   A pattern of attributes . . .

59

You'll see the screen acquire a complicated pattern of colours. (Note *how* the colours are painted in, always continuing to the end of their row at any given stage.) After a pause, the text goes in; see how the colours change whenever the text overprints a colour cell.

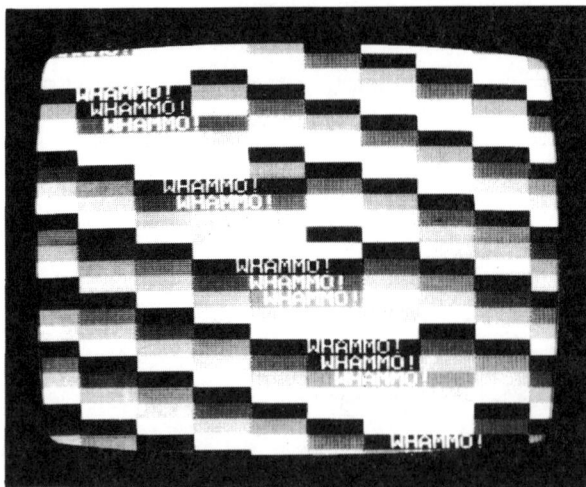

Figure 12.2   ... and how overprinting text cancels them.

Table 12.1

Code number	Attribute
0	Black INK
1	Red INK
2	Green INK
3	Yellow INK
4	Blue INK
5	Magenta INK
6	Cyan INK
7	White INK
8	Single height steady standard
9	Single height steady alternate
10	Double height steady standard
11	Double height steady alternate
12	Single height flashing standard
13	Single height flashing alternate
14	Double height flashing standard
15	Double height flashing alternate
16	Black PAPER
17	Red PAPER
18	Green PAPER
19	Yellow PAPER
20	Blue PAPER
21	Magenta PAPER
22	Cyan PAPER
23	White PAPER
24–31	Ignore—may affect screen synchronization

ATTRIBUTES

Those of you who have been wincing at the word 'colour' throughout can relax. There's a great deal more·to it than that. The PLOT C, R, T command actually sets an *attribute*—something that governs the way characters get printed. This can be an INK colour, a PAPER colour, or something like a FLASHING or DOUBLE HEIGHT command (of which more later). The attribute numbers run from 0 to 31. The *Manual* lists them in Appendix C, but in such an obscure way that I've given you a comprehensible list of the ones you may want to use in Table 12.1. For the alternate set and standard set of characters, see Chapter 19; for the use of double height characters see the next section. To see the effect of these attributes, try the following program with INPUTs of 0–23 in turn.

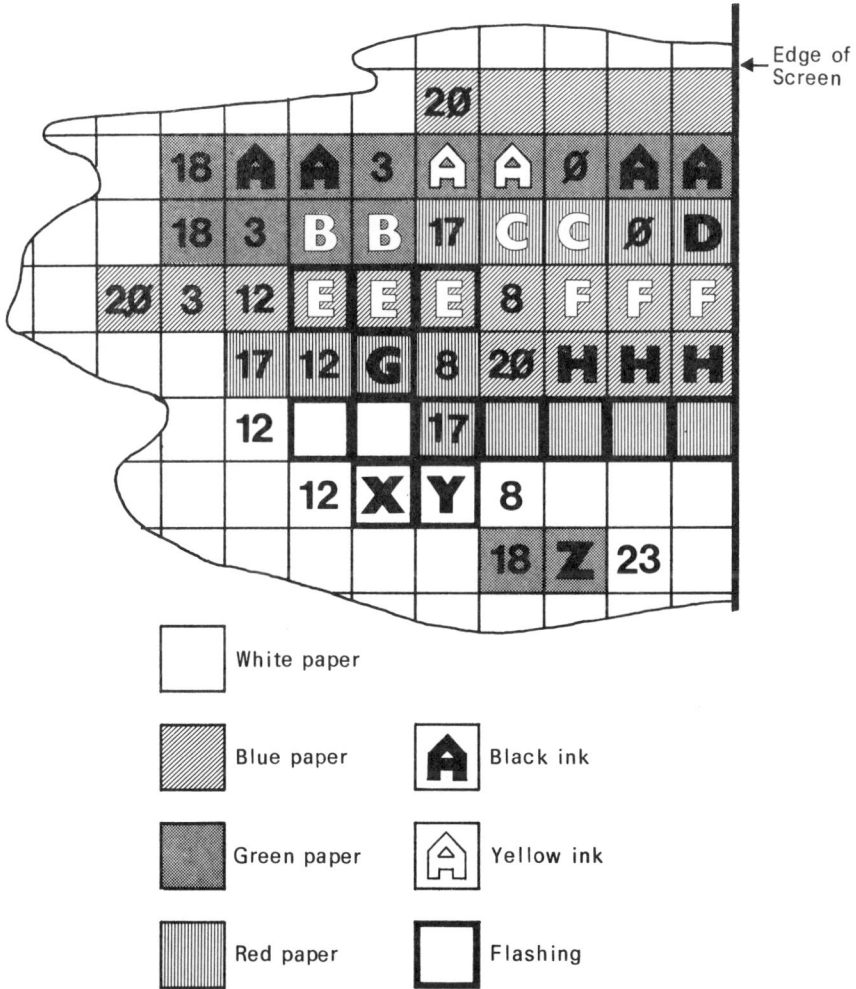

Figure 12.3   How serial attributes work. The numbers are attribute codes, the letters and blanks illustrate the effect on the screen. There are three groups: (a) INK colour, (b) PAPER colour, (c) flash, double height, standard/alternate. An attribute applies along its row until cancelled by one in the same group. The rows in the diagram exemplify different combinations.

```
 10  CLS
 20  REPEAT
 30  INPUT T
 40  UNTIL T > = 0 AND T < = 23
 50  PLOT 20, 9, "HELLO"
 60  PLOT 20, 10, "HELLO"
 70  WAIT 200
 80  PLOT 10, 9, T
 90  PLOT 10, 10, T
100  PRINT CHR$(30)
110  PRINT SPC(10)
120  PRINT CHR$(30)
130  GOTO 20
```

It's assembled from ideas already explained, so you can work through the listing for yourself to see how it operates.

Note that while the INK attribute codes correspond to the usual colour codes, the PAPER codes are 16 larger. Hence the T + 16 in the previous section (page 58).

DOUBLE HEIGHT AND FLASHING

You may have wondered why the previous program printed out 'HELLO' twice. It was to show the double height features. Since any double height character stretches over two rows, you need to PLOT the attribute on both rows; and you print out the letters on both so that it has something to attribute itself *to*. In fact, on an odd-numbered row the double

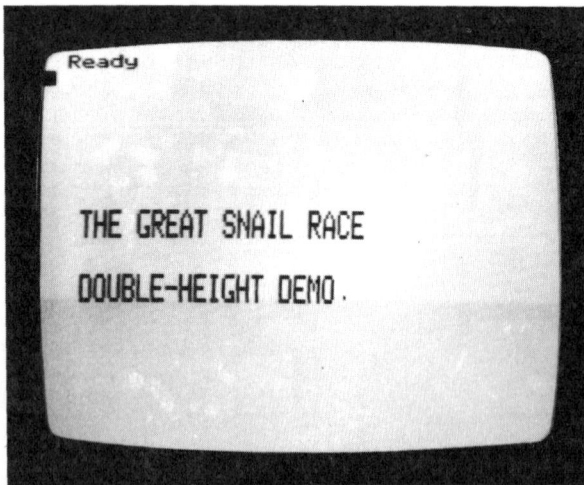

Figure 12.4   Demonstration of double height characters.

height attributes take the *top* half of a character and stretch it; on the even rows they take the bottom half. You need both to get the full character; and the top row has to be one with an *odd* number. Try this:

```
10  CLS
20  INPUT "PHRASE TO BE DOUBLED"; T$
30  INPUT "DOUBLE HEIGHT ROW NUMBER"; DR
40  FOR X = 2 * DR - 1 TO 2 * DR
50  PLOT 1, X, 10
60  PLOT 2, X, T$
70  NEXT X
80  GOTO 80
```

Input 'THE GREAT SNAIL RACE' and then row number 6, for a test. This facility is especially useful for giving a program a nice 'title page'.

The double height attribute is the 10 in line 50. (The FOR . . . NEXT just gets the odd/even doubled lines right.) If you change it to 14, you'll find that the words *flash*, as well.

You *can* use PLOT 0, X, 10 in line 50; but your ink colour turns *white* if you do.

Project 2

Write a program that produces on the screen a series of coloured rectangular frames, one inside the other, shrinking down to the centre. Figure 12.5 shows the kind of thing. [Hint: think of this as a series of nested rectangular blocks, with the smaller ones painted over the top of the bigger: start with the bigger ones and recall that attributes are serial, so that in each row you need only to switch a given colour on, and then off at some later place, to get a rectangular block of colour.]

Figure 12.5 Nested coloured rectangles for Project 2.

ANSWERS

Project 1

```
10   CLS
20   FOR P = 0 TO 7
30   PAPER(P)
40   WAIT 200
50   NEXT P
```

Project 2

```
10    CLS
20    FOR K = 0 TO 13
30    COL = K
40    IF COL > 7 THEN COL = COL − 8
50    CP = COL − 1
60    IF CP < 0 THEN CP = 7
70    FOR R = K TO 26 − K
80    PLOT K, R, COL + 16
90    PLOT 38 − K, R, CP + 16
100   NEXT R
110   NEXT K
120   GOTO 120
```

Once you've got a program working,
you can save it on tape and load
it back later: Here's how.

13 Using a Cassette Recorder

One of the first things you'll want to do with your Oric is to run the demonstration program. To do so, you'll need to connect up a cassette recorder. The supplied connecting lead has two 3-pin DIN connectors, so unless you want to take one end to bits and replace it with 3.5mm jacks, you need a recorder with a DIN socket. Most (but by no means all) do, so be careful if you're buying a new one for use with the Oric. I've tried three types with reasonable success:

Boots Audio CR 325
W.H. Smith CCR 800
Hitachi TRQ 295R

I say 'reasonable' success because, although each works independently, programs saved on one recorder do not necessarily load back successfully on one of the others. This probably won't matter to you, but if you want to load something on a friend's Oric it might be a good idea to take your recorder as well as the tape. The chances are that these problems arise because of slight differences in the azimuth adjustment of the recorder heads. If necessary, you can get a hi-fi shop to readjust this for you.

First, do a simple test. Connect the DIN cable to the recorder and the Oric. (The socket on the Oric is the one furthest from the aerial connector.)

Warning

Some recorders, the Hitachi among them, do not automatically disconnect the microphone when the DIN plug is inserted. In this case, you *must* insert a blanking plug (usually supplied for the purpose: if not, use a 3.5 mm jack plug without any leads) in the microphone (MIC) socket of the recorder.

CSAVE AND CLOAD

Now key in something quick and easy!

        10 REM AAAAAAAA

        20 REM BBBBBBBB

        30 REM CCCCCCCC

until you're fed up. (Don't take very long to get fed up. If it doesn't work you're just wasting time.)

Now type CSAVE"FRED" but don't hit RETURN yet. Start the recorder in RECORD mode and make sure that magnetic tape (not just plastic leader tape) is winding on to the take-up spool. Now hit RETURN. You'll see the message:

    Saving   FRED

appear on the top line of the display and then a little later:

Ready

When the 'Ready' prompt appears you can turn off the recorder and rewind the tape.
Set the volume control to about three quarters full on. Type CLOAD "FRED", hit
RETURN and PLAY the tape. The message:

Searching . . .

will appear on the display top line. If all is well, this will be replaced rapidly by:

Loading . . . FRED

and then a 'Ready' prompt.
Several things which can go wrong are:

1. The 'Loading . . .' message never occurs. This is because the volume setting is
   probably too high. (Of course, it could be too low, but you have to get very low before
   the Oric fails to detect SAVEd information.)
2. The 'Loading . . .' message occurs but is then followed by a 'FILE ERROR-LOAD
   ABORTED' message. This may be because the volume level is now too low, or the
   heads need cleaning. Put the recorder in PLAY mode so that the heads are exposed,
   and polish them gently with a cotton bud soaked in head-cleaning fluid. Then use a
   dry cotton bud to polish them off. Also clean the rubber pinch-roller in the same
   way, but be careful not to get the cotton bud close to the rotating capstan, or you may
   find the cotton unravelling round it, and it's then a pain to get off. (In other words
   brush the cotton bud lightly against the pinch-roller to the *right* of the capstan.)
   Another possibility is that the tape is poor quality, or has seen better days. In
   either case, the magnetic emulsion may have rubbed off in places and you can do
   nothing except resolve to use better tapes in future.

If the 'Loading . . .' message never occurs, you can hit the RESET button underneath the
Oric and as your program will still be in the machine you can try again.
If you've got a FILE ERROR message, the Oric will have loaded the program up to the
point where it noticed there was a problem. So you can LIST to see how much you've got,
and, with luck, patch up the problem by adding the last few (optimistic!) lines.
It is also possible for the Oric to believe it has loaded a program correctly when it's
actually misread a line. I recently loaded a program, and on attempting to run it was
immediately confronted with a syntax error message although the program had run
perfectly before! On investigation, it turned out that a PLAY command had mysteriously
become CIRCLE!

All being well, you should have squeaky-clean heads and a volume level which works. So now to the demo tape.

Type CLOAD " ", S

hit RETURN and PLAY the tape.

If you don't put anything between the quote marks (not even a space) the Oric will load the first program it comes across, whatever its name. (The name will *not* then appear in the loading message.) The ', S' tells the Oric that the program has been saved at a slow speed (in fact, about 30 characters/second), and so it does not try to read it back at the normal speed, which is about 240 characters/second. The theory is that programs saved in 'slow' mode are likely to be read back more reliably than those in the normal fast mode, although I can't say I've noticed the difference. If I have a loading problem, it's usually there, regardless of speed.

When there is more than one file on the tape you have to specify the name of the one you want between the quote marks. The Oric will then skip over unwanted ones. However, it doesn't tell you what's happening. The 'Searching . . .' message remains until the appropriate file is found. This can be a little disconcerting if you're not sure where a program is, or are worried about whether the tape is behaving itself.

The only way to provide yourself with some indication of what's going on is to listen to the tape. Don't do this via the loudspeaker unless you want burst eardrums. I leave a 'deaf aid' earpiece permanently connected to the external speaker socket of the cassette recorder.

Debugging I was about errors in 'grammar'. But a statement may be perfectly grammatical, yet produce nonsense in a program.

14 Debugging II

RUNTIME ERRORS

Although the Oric doesn't *actually* tell you about syntax errors until you type RUN, 1. principle it *could* do so, because all it needs to do is scan a statement to see that something is wrong. But there are other kinds of errors which can't possibly be identified until the program is run. These are called runtime errors.

Here's a simple example:

```
10   FOR P = 1 TO 20
20   N = 5 / (5 − P)
30   PRINT N
40   NEXT P
```

Run this. You'll find that it starts perfectly happily, and produces the values:

```
1.25
1.66666667
2.5
5
```

but then it generates an error message:

? DIVISION BY ZERO ERROR IN 20

So what's gone wrong? Well, the message tells us that the Oric has found something fishy about line 20 and that reads:

```
20   N = 5 / (5 − P)
```

Now, there can't be anything wrong with the statement itself because it has already been executed four times to produce the four numbers listed above. So it has to be something to do with the value of P which is the only thing that is changing. Type 'PRINT P' (or, to make things quicker, you can type '?P'). The screen displays '5'.

So the machine is trying to work out:

$$\frac{5}{5 - 5} = \frac{5}{0}$$

and it can't do that, because the result should be a number larger than any number you like to think of, and however big your Oric's memory is, it still wouldn't be able to hold it. So, very sensibly, the Oric notices when you try to divide something by zero, and simply won't attempt it, preferring to tell you that this is what has happened (by using the error code).

This error can crop up in much less obvious ways than this. How about this:

```
30  INPUT P, Q, R
40  A = (P + Q − R) / (5 + (P − R) * (P − R) − 2*Q)
```

Try 7, 15 and 2 as values for P, Q and R and see!

Project 1

What values would cause the 'division by zero' message in the following examples?

1. A = 7/(B − C)
2. R = P + Q/(2 * P − Q)
3. M = R + 2/(R * R + R * R * R)

ANSWERS

Project 1

You can get away with making all the variables zero in these examples, but other possibilities are:

1. Make B and C equal.
2. Make Q twice as big as P, e.g. Q = 7, P = 3.5.
3. Make R = − 1.

You *can* always (and always should) prevent the message arising by including a test of your own. For instance, in doing example 1 above, you could write:

```
20  INPUT B, C
30  D = B − C
40  IF D = 0 THEN PRINT "CAN'T DO THIS. TRY AGAIN": GOTO 20
50  A = 7/D
```

or:

```
20  REPEAT
30  INPUT B, C
40  D = B − C
50  UNTIL D < > 0
60  A = 7/D
```

Even an Oric can be unpredictable!

15 Random Numbers

In some programs you want the computer to behave in an unpredictable way. The Oric has a command that will produce 'random' numbers, and you can use these when you want it to do something, but you don't want to know in advance what it will do. This is especially useful in games: how many games can you think of that require the throw of a die or the drawing of a card?

The command for random numbers is:

RND

followed by a number in brackets. To get an idea of what this command will do, copy in and RUN the following program:

10   INPUT N
20   FOR T = 1 TO 10
30   PRINT RND(N)
40   NEXT T
50   GOTO 10

First, input 1 for N. You get ten decimal numbers between 0 and 1, with no obvious pattern. Try 1 again: you get more, still no pattern.

Now try 0. You get the same number ten times; moreoever it's the *same* as the last random number printed out when you used N = 1.

Now try −2. You get a number repeated ten times, but it's not the same as anything that's gone before.

In fact, the general result of RND(N) is this:

1. If N is positive, RND(N) generates random numbers between 0 and 1. (0 may occur, 1 will not.)
2. If N is zero, then RND(0) gives you whatever random number was generated previously. (Sometimes useful to work out where you are, if the program isn't storing the random numbers for you.)
3. If N is negative, RND(N) generates a *particular* 'random' number depending on N.

I suggest you ignore 3 altogether: it's mostly useful for debugging, and is related to the actual process whereby the 'random' numbers are produced. (They aren't really random, assuming that means anything; but the process that produces them is designed to give patternless results for most practical purposes.) In fact, the only command you'll ever be likely to need is:

RND(1)

and I'll stick to that from now on.

DICE, CARDS, AND GAMBLING DEVICES

Hang on, there's a knock at the door . . . No, Officer, I don't have a Gaming Licence . . . Well, since you insist, I'll change the section title to:

CHANCE EVENTS

Pheew! Now, to business. When you throw a die it produces numbers between 1 and 6, at random. The Oric's 'die' produces numbers between 0 and 1, which may be decimals. So a little mathematical jiggery-pokery (or, to maintain the gambling motif, piggery-pokery) is required.

Here's a typical list of random Oric numbers (in the first column) together with what happens when you multiply by 6.

RND(1)	6 * RND(1)
.131137465	.78682479
.80924873	4.85549238
.846447204	5.07868323
.591965711	5.04921935
.26800113	3.55179427

Now multiplying by 6 stretches the range of numbers 0–1 into 0–6. That's a step in the right direction. The next is to get rid of those decimals. The command:

INT

replaces a number by its *integer part:* the largest whole number not greater than it. For positive numbers this is the bit *before* the decimal point; for negative numbers it is 1 smaller. For instance:

INT(4.85549238) = 4

INT(−3.141592) = −4.

If there's nothing in front of the decimal point, INT gives 0 (for positive numbers). So if we take INTs of the right-hand column we get the sequence of numbers:

0   4   5   5   3

which are almost right for die-throws. The only snag is they run from 0 to 5 instead of 1 to 6. So we add 1:

1   5   6   6   4

and that's just right. Putting it all together we get:

INT(6 * RND(1)) + 1

which generates random whole numbers in the range 1–6, like a die.

Project 1

What commands would you use to generate random whole numbers corresponding to:

(a)   A pack of 52 cards?
(b)   A single suit of 13 cards?
(c)   A domino drawn from a full set of 28?
(d)   A birthday from a non-leap year?
(e)   A number between 10 and 99 (inclusive)?

71

FREQUENCY CHART

Here's a program of vaguely serious intent: it throws a die 150 times and records how many times each number comes up.

```
10   PAPER 0
20   INK 7
30   CLS
40   FOR R = 1 TO 6
50   PLOT 0, 3 * R, CHR$(48 + R)
60   NEXT R
70   FOR T = 1 TO 150
80   D = INT(6 * RND(1)) + 1
90   C(D) = C(D) + 1
100  IF C(D) > 36 THEN STOP
110  PLOT C(D) + 2, 3 * D, 16
120  PLOT C(D) + 1, 3 * D, 16 + D
130  NEXT T
140  GOTO 140
```

The number of times the die has thrown a number 1, 2, 3, 4, 5, 6 is recorded in six variables C(1), C(2), C(3), C(4), C(5), C(6). I've cheated a bit because this list of variables is what's called an *array*, and I'm not doing arrays until Chapter 21. No matter, the idea is clear enough.

Lines 40–60 print out the numbers 1–6 in a column. The CHR$(48 + R) just generates the characters for 1–6, whose codes (see Appendix D of the *Manual*) are 49–54.

Lines 70, 80, 130 throw the die 150 times.

Line 90 increases the count for the given throw.

Lines 110–120 use serial attributes to PLOT a block of colour on the screen in line with the number D. Line 100 just prevents the computer taking matters into its own hands if the PLOT position goes off the right-hand edge of the screen.

Note how the bars grow: although on a given run, one number may win, in the long run the wins even out. The Oric die is *fair*.

Project 2

Modify this program so that the computer throws *two* dice, each having only three sides (!) numbered 1, 2, 3 on one and 4, 5, 6 on the other; and adds the two scores. Do you expect the same results?

ANSWERS

Project 1

(a) INT(52 * RND(1)) + 1
(b) INT(13 * RND(1)) + 1
(c) INT(28 * RND(1)) + 1
(d) INT(365 * RND(1)) + 1
(e) INT(90 * RND(1)) + 10   (Because 90 * RND(1) runs from 0 to 89, so adding 10 gives the range 10–99. I got the 90 by counting the length of the range, 99 − 10 = 89 plus one on the end; then adjusted with the 10.)

You *may* have thought about doing the domino problem (c) by using INT(7 * RND(1)) to generate dots 0–6, with 0 standing for a blank domino (half). Do this twice; but keep only those pairs M, N for which M < = N, otherwise you'll get the non-doubled dominoes like ⟦3⟧6⟧, twice, once this way and once as ⟦6⟧3⟧; but the doubles ⟦5⟧5⟧ only once, and that changes the probabilities.

Project 2

```
 10   PAPER 0
 20   INK 7
 30   CLS
 40   FOR R = 1 TO 5
 50   PLOT 0, 3 * R, CHR$(52 + R)
 60   NEXT R
 70   FOR T = 1 TO 150
 80   D = INT(3 * RND(1)) + 1 + INT(3 * RND(1)) + 4
 90   C(D) = C(D) + 1
100   IF C(D) > 36 THEN STOP
110   PLOT C(D) + 2, 3 * D – 12, 16
120   PLOT C(D) + 1, 3 * D – 12, 12 + D
130   NEXT T
140   GOTO 140
```

The dice-throws come in line 80. Everything else adjusts for the fact that the total (1, 2, or 3) + (4, 5, or 6) must lie in the range 5–9.

Theoretically, you can get the following combinations:

Second die

		4	5	6	
	1	5	6	7	
First die	2	6	7	8	total
	3	7	8	9	

So in the long run, we expect a total of 7 for 1/3 of the throws, 6 or 8 for 2/9, and 5 or 9 for 1/9 of them. So that bar chart's rows ought to be in the approximate sizes 1:2:3:2:1 and form a sort of triangle. Do they?

Computers can be made to manipulate words,
or other kinds of symbolic notation,
as well as numbers.

16 Strings

The postman knocketh . . . with a letter. For *you*. A very personal letter. 'Dear Mr Slugshaver,' it says, 'You have been selected from the people of Lower Pigpen to receive, absolutely free of charge . . .'

Very gratifying. But next door, old Mrs Snagglechest has received the very same letter. In fact, the whole of Lower Pigpen has, along with most of the West Midlands.

Here's how it's done.

```
 10   INPUT "WHAT IS YOUR NAME"; N$
 20   INPUT "WHAT TOWN DO YOU LIVE IN"; T$
 30   CLS
 40   PRINT "DEAR MR ▽"; N$
 50   PRINT "▽▽▽ YOU HAVE BEEN SELECTED FROM"
 60   PRINT "THE PEOPLE OF ▽"; T$
 70   PRINT "TO RECEIVE, ABSOLUTELY FREE OF"
 80   PRINT "CHARGE (*), A MAGNIFICENT"
 90   PRINT "MOULDED SOYA GARDEN PATH."
100   PRINT "▽▽▽ WE ARE SURE, MR ▽"; N$
110   PRINT "THAT YOU WILL BE LED RIGHT"
120   PRINT "UP IT."
130   PRINT "▽▽▽▽ YOURS SINCERELY,"
140   PRINT "▽▽▽▽▽▽ MILTON F. GNATBENDER"
150   PRINT "▽▽▽▽▽▽ DEALER'S WRY JEST."
160   PRINT
170   PRINT "* POSTAGE $1066 EXTRA"
```

Run this, and choose your inputs:

SLUGSHAVER
LOWER PIGPEN

MOUSEBENDER
GOAT END

and so forth. Try other names and towns. Hmmmmmmm . . .

Now imagine this automatically fed names and addresses from a data bank, churning out thousands of letters an hour.

The interesting thing, apart from how blatant the whole exercise is, is that absolutely no *computation* is involved. Merely memory, and some very simple manipulation of written text. The computer can manage this because, as well as numbers, it can store *strings*. That's what those dollar signs $ signal, though there may be some Freudian significance too in the present context.

I've already introduced strings and string variables in Chapter 6. Now I'll show you how to manipulate them, starting with:

CONCATENATION

... which is a fancy word for 'sticking together'. To jam two strings end to end you write a + sign between them. For example,

PRINT "HOT" + "DOG"

which yields:

HOTDOG

Notice the order: "DOG + "HOT" gives 'DOGHOT'. Note also that the quotes are not *part* of the string: when a string is printed or otherwise manipulated, the quotes are there only to say where the ends are.

You can combine several strings together in this way:

10   INPUT B$, C$

20   PRINT B$ + B$ + C$

What happens if you try:

B$ = "B"   C$ = "C"

B$ = "CO"   C$ = "NUT"

B$ = "BYE▽"   C$ = "BLACKBIRD"

as inputs? Why?

If a particular sequence of characters (and that *includes* graphic characters) occurs several times in a program, you may find it worth while assigning it to a string variable.

THE LENGTH OF A STRING

The command:

LEN

yields the *length* of a string—that is, the number of characters in it. For instance,

LEN("FIDO") = 4

LEN("£££££££££££") = 11

LEN("2 + 2 = 5") = 5

LEN(" ") = 0

where " ", the *empty string,* is a string with *no* characters in it. In general, to find the length of string K$, you ask for:

LEN(K$)

To test this out, try this program:

```
10   INPUT "STRING"; K$
20   PRINT K$; "∇ HAS LENGTH"; LEN(K$)
30   GOTO 10
```

It should be self-explanatory.

WORD-REVERSAL

The next program accepts as input a word, letter by letter, and uses string concatenation to produce the same word but in reverse. (By using more advanced commands like MID$, LEFT$, RIGHT$, it would be possible to input the whole word in one go, but for simplicity I'll take it one letter at a time here. See the next chapter for more details.)

```
10   INPUT "FIRST LETTER?"; F$
20   INPUT "NEXT LETTER?"; N$
30   IF N$ = "0" THEN 60
40   F$ = N$ + F$
50   GOTO 20
60   CLS
70   PRINT F$
```

To stop the inputs, in line 20, enter '0' instead of a letter.

To see how this works, consider the word 'YELLOW'. In line 10 we input the first letter, 'Y', and so F$ is set to 'Y'. Then in line 20 we input the next letter 'E'. Line 40 now changes F$ to:

$$N\$ + F\$ = "E" + "Y" = "EY"$$

and line 50 sends us back to 20 for another letter, this time 'L'. So F$ then becomes:

$$N\$ + F\$ = "L" + "EY" = "LEY"$$

and so on:

Input 'L': F$ = N$ + F$ = 'L' + "LEY" = "LLEY"

Input 'O': F$ = N$ + F$ = "O" + "LLEY" = "OLLEY"

Input 'W': F$ = N$ + F$ = "W" + "OLLEY" = "WOLLEY"

Input '0': Program jumps to line 60 and prints 'WOLLEY'

The crucial point is the order in which the strings are added in line 40. What happens if you write:

```
40   F$ = F$ + N$
```

instead?

Project 1

There is a word-game in which the first player makes up a simple sentence such as:

YESTERDAY I SAW A BABOON

The next player adds an adjective describing the baboon:

YESTERDAY I SAW A PINK BABOON

The next adds another adjective:

YESTERDAY I SAW A FIERCE PINK BABOON

and so on, with the sentence getting longer and longer (until someone forgets which word comes where), ending up with something like:

YESTERDAY I SAW A SCRUPULOUS LAZY GULLIBLE FRAGRANT REFRESHING ENORMOUS PARTICULAR REINFORCED DISGRUNTLED PLASTIC DISTINGUISHED FIERCE PINK BABOON

or whatever.

Write a program to let players build up such sentences by inputting the extra adjective at each stage.

ANSWERS

Project 1

```
10  Y$ = "YESTERDAY I SAW A▽"
20  B$ = "BABOON"
30  A$ = " "
40  PRINT Y$ + A$ + B$
50  INPUT "ADJECTIVE?"; I$
60  A$ = I$ + "▽" + A$
70  GOTO 40
```

By picking out portions of a string, to get substrings, you can manipulate words. Examples given here include computer Spoonerisms, and a program to tell you what day of the week your birthday was.

17 Substrings

In the previous chapter I introduced the idea of a *string* of characters. Now I'm going to talk about the commands:

LEFT$

RIGHT$

MID$

which let you select portions of a string—*substrings*. These are very useful commands for general string-handling.

LEFT, RIGHT AND CENTRE

To select the left-hand end of a string, you use the command:

LEFT$(X$, N)

which gives the leftmost N characters of the string X$. For example,

10 LET X$ = "TEMPERATURE CHART"

20 LET Y$ = LEFT$(X$, 6)

30 PRINT Y$

gives TEMPER. Similarly there is a command for the right-hand N characters:

RIGHT$(X$, N)

and

10 LET X$ = "TEMPERATURE CHART"

20 LET Y$ = RIGHT$(X$, 3)

30 PRINT Y$

yields ART. (Incidentally, those LETs are optional, and can be left out just as for assignments of numeric variables.)

Finally in this order of ideas, there is a command:

MID$(X$, M, N)

which gives the N characters of X$ that start at position M. There is a restriction on M: it must be greater than ∅. If N is left out, everything from position M onwards is included. In the above, if you put:

    20   LET Y$ = MID$(X$, 6, 3)

you get RAT.

    A typical use of this is to print the day of the week, given a number (1 to 7 starting with Sunday):

    10   W$ = "SUNMONTUEWEDTHUFRISAT"

    20   INPUT "WHICH DAY?"; D

    30   Y$ = MID$(W$, 3 * D − 2, 3)

    40   PRINT Y$

The 3 * D − 2 gives the correct starting positions 1, 4, 7, 10, 13, 16 and 19 in W$.

Project 1

Use a string "JANFEBMAR . . . DEC" to write a similar program to print out the month, given a number from 1 to 12.

STRINGS AND NUMBERS

The string "493" and the number 493 are considered to be different by the computer. You may not notice this if you just print them:

    PRINT 493

    PRINT "493"

give the same result. Now try:

    PRINT 493 + 7

    PRINT "493" + 7

    PRINT "493" + "7"

You'll find you get three different results:

    500

    ? TYPE MISMATCH ERROR

    4937

    In the first case, it just adds the numbers.

    In the second, it tries to add a string to a number, getting a *type mismatch*, which just means it can't be done. (What should "CATCH" + 22 be? Well, maybe that's not the best example after all . . . .)

    In the third, it concatenates the strings "493" and "7" to get "4937" and then prints without the quotes.

    This can be very useful, because you can do things with strings that aren't so easy with numbers. For example, to find the first digit of 987654321 you just need LEFT$("987654321", 1). With arithmetical methods, it's a lot harder. *But* the result would be a *string* "9" and not the number 9. Now maybe you want to do some arithmetic with that 9. How?

    A string which happens to be in the form of a number (with quotes round it) can be turned into a bona fide number by using the command word:

    VAL

(for 'value'). So:

VAL("9")

is the *number* 9. Try:

PRINT VAL("493") + VAL("7")

and you'll see it really does work.

There is a similar command:

STR$

that works the other way round: it converts a number to a string. For example:

STR$(7751) is "7751"

COMPUTER SPOONERISMS

The Reverend W. A. Spooner was notorious for his habit of interchanging the front ends of pairs of words, often to comic effect; so that instead of:

FORMLESS WISH

he would say:

WORMLESS FISH

and so on.

By using string-manipulations it is possible to get the computer to generate Spoonerisms. Whether they are funny, or not, is firstly a matter of taste, and secondly, up to the user to decide. The program has no opinions on the matter. Here it is:

```
10   INPUT "FIRST WORD"; A$
20   INPUT "SECOND WORD"; B$
30   P$ = LEFT$(A$, 1)
40   Q$ = MID$(A$, 2)
```

```
50   R$ = LEFT$(B$, 1)

60   S$ = MID$(B$, 2)

70   PRINT A$ + "∇" + B$

80   PRINT "SPOONERIZED BECOMES:"

90   PRINT R$ + Q$ + "∇" + P$ + S$

100  GOTO 10
```

Run this, and input "FLYING" and "PIG" in lines 10 and 20.

Now line 30 takes the first character on the left of "FLYING", so P$ = "F". And line 40 takes everything from character 2 onwards, making Q$ = "LYING". Then line 50 gives R$ = "P"; and line 60 gives S$ = "IG".

Lines 70 and 80 set up the original word and suitable output messages; and line 90 prints out:

"P" + "LYING" + "∇" + "F" + "IG" = PLYING FIG

which isn't so bad, considering.

DAYFINDER

This program accepts as input a date (day number D, month M, year Y) and works out which day of the week it is.


```
10   A$ = "033614625035"

20   B$ = "SUNMONTUEWEDTHUFRISAT"

30   INPUT "DAY"; D

40   INPUT "MONTH"; M

50   INPUT "YEAR"; Y

60   PRINT "THE DAY IS∇";

70   Z = Y − 1

80   C = INT(Z/4) − INT(Z/100) + INT(Z/400)

90   X = Y + D + C + VAL(MID$(A$, M, 1)) − 1

100  IF M > 2 AND (Y = 4 * INT(Y/4) AND
     Y < > 100 * INT(Y/100) OR Y = 400 *
     INT(Y/400)) THEN X = X + 1

110  X = X − 7 * INT(X/7)

120  PRINT MID$(B$, 3 * X + 1, 3)
```


Copy this out *very* carefully, especially the brackets in line 100. Run it, and input (as a test) 24 for D, 9 for M and 1945 for Y. (That is, 24th September 1945. You *must* input the full year and not just 45, or the program gets the wrong answer.) You should get:

THE DAY IS MON

for Monday. Try today's date. Try your birthday. Find out what date Anne Boleyn died, and try that.

Line 10 stores twelve 'monthly correction numbers' in compact form as a single string.
Line 20 sets up the 'day-of-the-week' string described above.
Lines 30–60 are input/output statements, nothing unusual.

Lines 80–100 perform a complicated calculation that takes into account leap years and the 'monthly corrections'. Note the use of VAL and MID$ in line 90; what it actually does here is to find the Mth digit in A$ and convert it to a number.

Line 110 produces a number in the range 0–6 for the day of the week (rather than the 1–7 used above in the illustration); and line 120 prints out the day itself using MID$ on B$.

ANSWERS

Project 1

```
10   M$ = "JANFEBMARAPRMAYJUNJULAUGSEPOCTNOVDEC"
20   INPUT "WHICH MONTH"; M
30   Y$ = MID$(M$, 3 * M − 2, 3)
40   PRINT Y$
```

Pencil and paper still have their uses . . .

18 Debugging III

DRY RUN TABLES

More often than not, runtime errors aren't as easy to find as those in Debugging II. If you can't see what's wrong straight away, you need to check the coding in a careful and systematic way. It can be a rather laborious process, but if you stick to it rigidly, it's almost guaranteed to pay off.

I'll explain the techniques of 'dry running' a program with an example. We'll imagine you've found the following piece of code in a magazine article:

```
10   INPUT "ENTER NEXT NO."; N
20   IF N > 0 THEN S = S + N: C = C + I: GOTO 10
30   PRINT "AVERAGE IS"; S/C
40   INPUT "ANY MORE DATA (Y/N)"; Q$
50   IF Q$ = "Y" THEN 10
```

and the associated text tells you that this will find the average of a set of positive numbers, terminated by zero. In other words you could enter:

ENTER NEXT NO. ? 3

ENTER NEXT NO. ? 4

ENTER NEXT NO. ? 5

ENTER NEXT NO. ? 0

and it should come up with the message:

AVERAGE IS 4

(The zero is not part of the data; it is the delimiter, see Chapter 8). The program will then ask the user if he wants to deal with another data set:

ANY MORE DATA (Y/N)?

If you type 'Y' in response to this question, the program will start all over again asking for a new set of numbers.

If you key the program in and run it with the numbers 3, 4, 5 and 0, you'll find that it doesn't work. It accepts the numbers as you'd expect but when you've entered the zero, it crashes with the message:

? DIVISION BY ZERO ERROR IN 30

The zero gremlin has struck again!

Now, to find out what the silly machine has done, you pretend you *are* the machine and obey, slavishly, the program instructions as the machine would. You show how the various values the program handles change in a table like this:

Line No.	S	N	C	I	Branch

There are only four variables in this program: S, N, C and I. As every line is executed you enter the line number, the new values of S, N, C and I (if they are changed on that line) and, if the statement is an IF . . . THEN, a tick in the Branch column if a jump occurs, a cross otherwise.

Before we start though, there's one thing the Oric will do as soon as you type RUN, and that is to zero all variables, so the table actually appears like this to start with:

Line No.	S	N	C	I	Branch
	0	0	0	0	

Suppose we test the program on the numbers 3, 4, 5 and 0. The first time line 10 is executed, 3 will be passed to N, so:

Line No.	S	N	C	I	Branch
10	0	0 3	0	0	

At line 20, N is greater than zero, so the 3 is added to S, I (0) is added to C, and the branch to line 10 does take place:

Line No.	S	N	C	I	Branch
10	0	0 3	0	0	
20	3		0		✓

Continuing the process we get:

Line No.	S	N	C	I	Branch
10	0	0 3	0	0	
20	3		0		✓
10		4			
20	7		0		✓
10		5			
20	12		0		✓
10		0			
20					✗
30					← attempt to evaluate 12/0

So we can see why the 'DIVISION BY ZERO' error has cropped up. Now we can use the table to give some clues about how each variable is changing. Look at the N column first. We can see the 3, 4, 5 and 0 which were input appearing in turn, which is what you'd expect. S is more interesting. Here we can see the sum of the numbers in N gradually being formed. First the 3 appears, then 7 (3 + 4), then 12 (3 + 4 + 5). But what about C? Absolutely nothing is happening to it! Since three numbers have been entered, the average should be 12/3 = 4, so C ought to be 3. Actually, the reason C remains at zero is that it keeps having I added to it and I is fixed at zero. Suppose I is a misprint for 1? Then the table would look like this:

Line No.	S	N	C	Branch	
	0	0	0		
10		3			
20	3		1	√	
10		4			
20	7		2	√	
10		5			
20	12		3	√	
10		0			
20				×	
30					Print 12/3 = 4

So now things look promising. Edit line 20 to change the 'I' to a '1' and RUN. Enter 3, 4, 5, 0 as before and 4 is displayed. So far so good. Now enter 'Y' when you're asked if there's any more data, and try 10, 20, 30, 0. The program prints out the answer 12, which is odd because the average of 10, 20 and 30 is 20!

LOGICAL ERRORS

Now this is an example of a new kind error—a logical error. The program does something, and completes its task without the Oric noticing anything wrong, but whatever it was that the program did, it was *not* to take the average of 10, 20 and 30.

So let's continue the dry run table to see what's gone wrong. There's little point in repeating the work done so far, so we can just note that, when we reach line 40, S = 12, N = 0 and C = 3. Also, we now need the string variable Q$:

Line No.	S	N	C	Q$	Branch
40	12	0	3	Y	
50					√
10		10			
20	22		4		

I don't think we need go any further to see the problem. Since S is 12 to start with, it becomes 22 when it should only be 10, and C becomes 4 when it should be 1. In other words the Oric hasn't forgotten the first set of values when it processes the second, so it will work out:

$$(3 + 4 + 5 + 10 + 20 + 30)/6 = 12$$

Now it's easy to deal with; simply include a line 5:

    5   S = 0: C = 0

and edit line 50 to read:

    50   IF Q$ = "Y" THEN 5

How likely are the kinds of errors we've seen here? Well, printing errors of the I for 1, 2 for Z type are fairly common (although not in this book, I hope), and even if the error isn't on the printed page, it's quite likely you'll make the odd transcription error without noticing it when you're keying in a program. Even when you're writing a program of your own, you'd be surprised how often you can forget the name of a variable and use the wrong one, or even use the same variable for two different things. You should be careful, and note the name of every variable and what its function is as you invent it, but human nature being what it is . . .

The second error shows up two important things. First, although BASIC is trying to be helpful by initializing variables to zero without you asking it to do so, it's something of a mixed blessing. It's good practice to set up all variables at the beginning of a program even though you may not need to do so, because it avoids the possibility of a mistake like this one. I'm not suggesting that you are likely to make an error as trivial as this one, but if a program is written to deal with one set of data, and only later is it altered to handle many sets, you can see how initializations could be forgotten.

Secondly it illustrates how careful you must be when testing a program. Just because a program works for one set of data, you mustn't jump to the conclusion that it will work just as well for every other possible set.

Project 1

Here's an example for you to try your skills on. The following program is supposed to accept a sequence of positive values (zero up to 1000) and, at the end, print out the largest and smallest values it has read. A negative number is used as a delimiter. For instance, if the data are 8, 4, 3, 9, −1 the program should print out:

    9   3

I'll give you one clue—there are two errors to look for.

    10   MAX = 0: MIN = 0
    20   INPUT N
    30   IF N < MIN THEN MIN = N
    40   IF N > MAX THEN MAX = N
    50   IF N < 0 THEN PRINT MAX, MIN: END
    60   GOTO 20

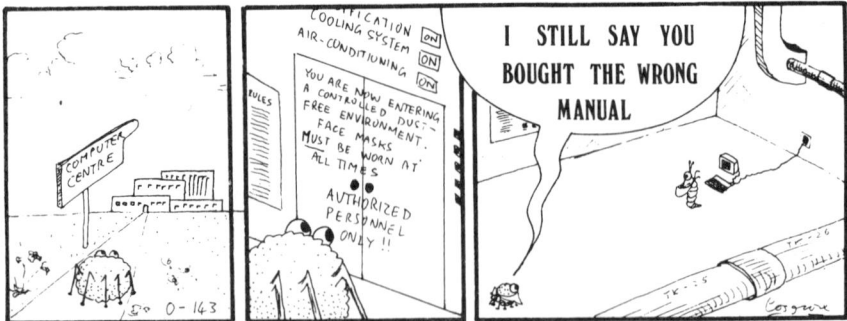

I STILL SAY YOU BOUGHT THE WRONG MANUAL

ANSWER

Project 1

With my example dataset the dry run table will look like this:

Line No.	MAX	MIN	N	Branch
	0	0	0	
10	0	0		
20			8	
30				
40	8			
50				
60				
20			4	
30				
40				
50				
60				
20			3	
30				
40				
50				
60				√
20			9	
30				
40	9			
50				
60				√
20			−1	
30		−1		
40				
50				Print 9, −1

So the *largest* value is being correctly printed but the smallest isn't. Looking down the MAX column we can see how the program is supposed to work. Every time a value larger than that in MAX at the moment comes along, it replaces the current value in MAX. MIN should, of course, behave in a similar way so that first 8, then 4, then 3 should appear there. But no changes occur in MIN until −1 is entered and that isn't supposed to affect things at all, since it's only the delimiter!

The reason that no new values are being placed in MIN is that there's the smallest possible value (zero) already in it. MIN should start with a very large value in it so that the first value to come along will replace it, because the new value is *bound* to be smaller. Since the largest possible value is known to be 1000, *anything* greater than this will do. So line 10 becomes:

    10   MAX = 0: MIN = 1001

Now we must prevent the delimiting −1 getting into MIN. That's easy. We must ask if the end of the data has been reached before trying to transfer the value to MAX or MIN. So line 50 should be deleted and rewritten as line 25.

There are two different levels of graphics on the Oric. The coarsest builds up shapes by using a selection of special characters to draw tiny blocks.

19 The Art of Coarse Graphics

As well as TEXT, the low-resolution screen can display graphics. It uses the same Text Screen arrangement (27 rows of 40 cells numbered in columns 0–38 and rows 0–26, plus a reserved column at far left as in Figure 9.1); but uses two new mode-setting commands:

> LORES0
>
> LORES1

(The word is LO-RES, short for LOw RESolution, and has nothing to do with Folk Tales or lawyers who can't spell.) These differ only in the way that character-printing commands are interpreted.

ASCII CODES

Every Oric character has a code number, its ASCII Code. (The letters stand for American Standard Code for Information Interchange.) The codes are listed in Appendix D of the *Manual.* You can ask for a character by name:

> PRINT "A"

or by code:

> PRINT CHR$(65)

because the ASCII code for "A" is 65. In general:

> CHR$(N)

gives the character whose ASCII code is the number N. Conversely you can find out the code for a character by asking for:

ASC(character).

So ASC("A") is 65. The codes actually run from 0 to 255, but standard ASCII uses only 32–125, which are listed in Appendix D. To see what happens with the other numbers, try this:

```
10   INPUT N
20   PRINT CHR$(N)
30   GOTO 10
```

In particular try 126 as in input: it's quite a useful character. Some codes can lead to the screen going out of synch: if this happens use the RESET button underneath.

Project 1

What effect do you get by adding 128 to the codes in Appendix D of the *Manual?*

LORES0: THE STANDARD SET

In LORES0 mode, the computer uses the standard set of characters. In fact, LORES0 is rather similar to TEXT mode (Chapters 5, 9); but there are a few crucial differences.
First, when it is first set up, the PAPER is black and the INK white.
Second, the command:

PLOT X, Y, C

used to set attributes in Chapter 12, appears to affect only the cell at position X, Y. (Otherwise it functions as in TEXT mode.) For instance, this program plots random colours to the screen:

```
10   LORES0
20   C = 39 * RND(1)
30   R = 27 * RND(1)
40   COLOUR = 8 * RND(1) + 16
50   PLOT C, R, COLOUR
60   GOTO 20
```

And this one jazzes that idea up, to produce random rectangles and a rather pretty Modern Art design:

```
10   LORES0
20   REPEAT
30   RT = 27 * RND(1)
40   RB = RT + 10 * RND(1)
50   UNTIL RB < = 26
60   REPEAT
70   CL = 39 * RND(1)
80   CR = CL + 10 * RND(1)
90   UNTIL CR < = 38
```

```
100   COLOUR = 16 + 8 * RND(1)
110   FOR C = CL TO CR
120   FOR R = RT TO RB
130   PLOT C, R, COLOUR
140   NEXT R
150   NEXT C
160   GOTO 20
```

Note the two REPEAT . . . UNTIL loops, which make sure PLOT points don't go off screen; the use of RND(1) for randomness; and the FOR . . . NEXT loop to plot the rectangles.

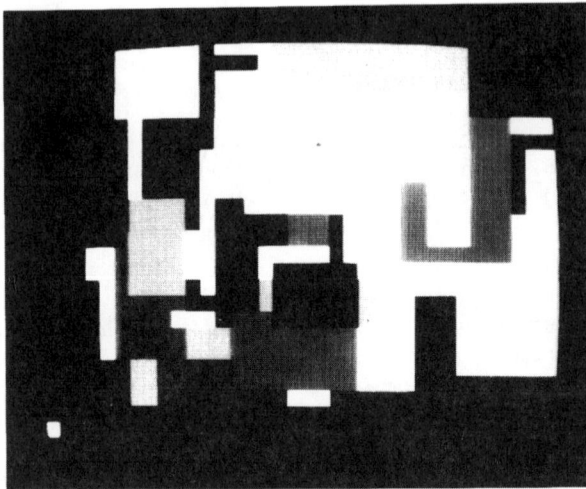

Figure 19.1   Modern Art.

Project 2

This is like Project 1, but in LORES0 and using PLOT. Type this in:

```
10   LORES0
20   INPUT N
30   PLOT 5, 5, CHR$(N)
40   GOTO 20
```

Now what happens if you add 128 to the ASCII code of a standard character such as 'A'?

LORES1: ALTERNATE SET

The LORES1 mode is almost the same as LORES0, *except* that the entire character set changes. Every program instruction that refers to a character, either directly or via the ASCII code, produces the corresponding character from the *alternate set*. For example, key this in:

```
10   LORES1
20   PRINT "ABCDE"
30   PRINT "FGHIJ"
40   PRINT "KLMNO"
50   PRINT "PQRST"
60   PRINT "UVWXY"
70   GOTO 70
```

Instead of the letters, you get a rather peculiarly shaped *thing*, like Figure 19.2.

Figure 19.2   Alternate characters yield unfamiliar results from familiar commands.

The letters from the standard character set have been systematically replaced by characters from the alternate set. Mostly, these are chunky block graphics shapes, known as *teletext* characters because they are compatible with TV Teletext systems like Oracle. The Oric *Manual* doesn't say which characters are which, so I've listed them for you in Appendix 2. You can also list them out systematically by using the program in Project 2 but with line 10 replaced by LORES1.

You'll find that while you are in LORES1, anything you type comes out in Chunky Nutritious Teletext, at least until the screen starts scrolling. To get out of this state, type:

CLS

directly: ignore the printout on screen!

You can change INK colour within LORES1; but not PAPER colour (or you lose the alternate characters). After a scroll you may find that an initial CLS before the LORES1 command helps. The reason for all this would seem to be that the LORES1 command sets up *attributes* in the reserved column of screen, telling the machine to use the alternate set. PAPER mucks these up, and scrolls shift them up the screen.

Sometimes when a program in LORES1 crashes, the error message is printed in the alternate character set and you can't read it. If so, type:

PAPER 0

in direct mode (and ignore what you see on the screen) to recover the standard set.

SKYLINES

The next program shows how you can mix colours on the screen by setting different attributes in different positions. It generates a random futuristic city skyline.

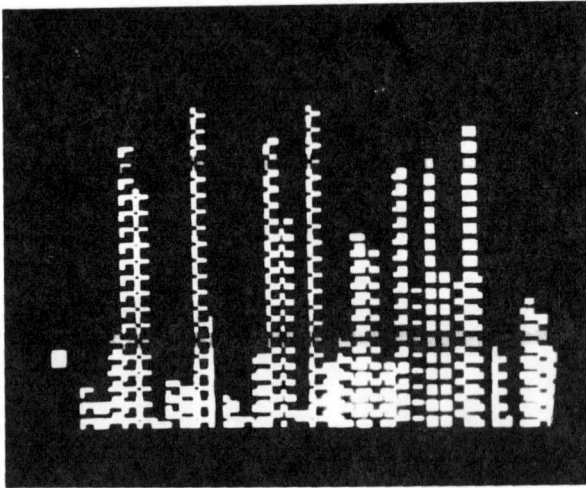

Figure 19.3   Typical screen plot from Skylines.

```
 10   LORES1
 20   FOR R = 0 TO 26
 30   PLOT 0, R, 1 + 7 * RND(1)
 40   NEXT R
 50   FOR C = 1 TO 38
 60   X = 32 + 64 * RND(1)
 70   RT = 26 − 20 * RND(1)
 80   FOR R = 26 TO RT STEP −1
 90   PLOT C, R, CHR$(X)
100   NEXT R
110   NEXT C
120   GOTO 120
```

Line 10 sets up the alternate character set. Lines 20–40 place random INK colour attributes in column 0. Line 60 chooses a random alternate character; line 70 a random height for the skyscraper in column C. Lines 80–100 draw the skyscraper from the bottom up; and 50 and 110 loop the column to get a whole skyline.

Project 3

Change line 70 to:

```
 70   RT = 26 − 20 * ABS(SIN(C/5))
```

and see what shape you get. (For ABS and SIN see the *Manual* pages 56 and 71: maths has its uses after all!)

92

BLOCK GRAPHICS

To all intents and purposes you should think of the teletext characters as living in a 3×3 grid, so that 'A' corresponds to Figure 19.4, and so on. (Strictly, it's a 6×8 grid, with the 6 grouped 2/2/2 and the 8 grouped 3/2/3, but that's splitting hairs.) So you can assemble pictures out of block graphics by drawing on a grid.

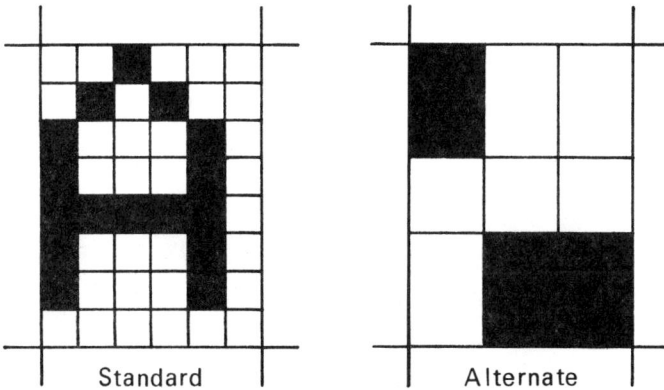

Standard   Alternate

Figure 19.4   Standard and alternate characters with code 65. There is no special relation between one set and the other.

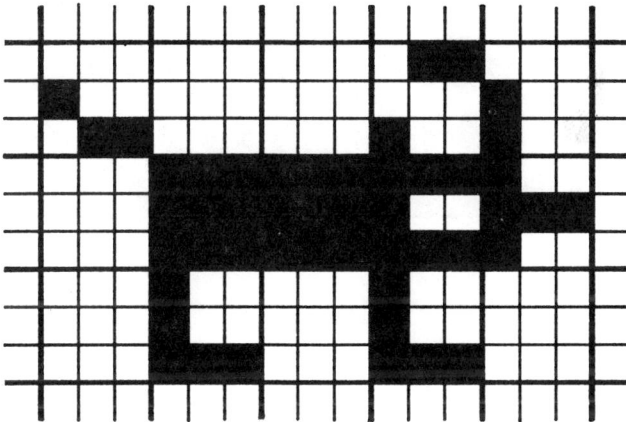

Figure 19.5   Eric the Nannygoat in Lo-res Graphics.

I don't know what an Oric looks like, but maybe it's a bit like a goat*. I've drawn a chunky goat in Figure 19.5 and broken her up into 3×3 sub-blocks. These turn out (from Appendix 2) to correspond to the standard characters whose codes are:

68	32	32	50	52
32	95	95	87	61
32	85	32	85	32

These are:

D	▽	▽	2	4
▽	£	£	W	=
▽	U	▽	U	▽

*Yes I do—it's the little man with a square head in the *Manual*. Personally, I'd rather have a goat . . .

So I can print out my goat (actually, she's called Eric, which is close enough, though the vet needs his eyes tested) like this:

```
10   CLS
20   LORES1
30   INK 2              (for a green goat)
40   PRINT "D▽▽24"
50   PRINT "▽££W ="
60   PRINT "▽U▽U▽"
70   GOTO 70
```

Figure 19.6   Looping Eric to get a flock of goats. What? Herd of goats? Of course I've heard of goats!

ANSWERS

Project 1

Absolutely none.

Project 2

Video-inversion: INK and PAPER change round.

IT'S AMAZING WHAT PEOPLE WILL PUT UP WITH FOR A JOB IN TELEVISION ...

Cosgrove

O-135

Project 3

See Figure 19.7. .

Figure 19.7   Trigonometric Skyline.

*By printing the same characters
in different positions, you can
produce the illusion of movement.
And the movements can be
controlled from the keyboard.*

20 Moving Graphics

Next, I'll make Eric the nannygoat *move*. I'll do this by printing her in lots of different places. Here's the first (failed) attempt:

```
10   CLS
20   LORES1
30   INK 3                        (yellow goats this time)
40   FOR C = 1 TO 30
50   PLOT C, 10, "D∇∇24"
60   PLOT C, 11, "∇££W="
70   PLOT C, 12, "∇U∇U∇"
80   NEXT C
90   GOTO 90
```

Nearly, right: but Eric's tail seems to streeeeeeeetch somewhat . . . Of course: I've left traces of previous goats littered about the screen.

Without doubt the neatest way to take care of this is to equip Eric with an extra 'invisible tail' of blank spaces, which will follow along behind her and wipe out unwanted junk. (Legend has is that the *fox* erases his tracks with his tail: in the Age of the Computer, so do goats). Modify the following lines (a good chance to practise your editing) and leave the rest as before:

```
50   PLOT C, 10, "∇D∇∇24"
60   PLOT C, 11, "∇∇££W="
70   PLOT C, 12, "∇∇U∇U∇"
```

All I've done is put an extra space in each of the three strings that build up the goat.

Project 1

Use the grid in Figure 20.1 to produce a dog. Make it move along the screen from *right to left*.

A word of warning: not all combinations of squares in a 3 × 3 grid are available in the alternate character set (you'd need 512 of them to do that) so you should select your designs carefully.

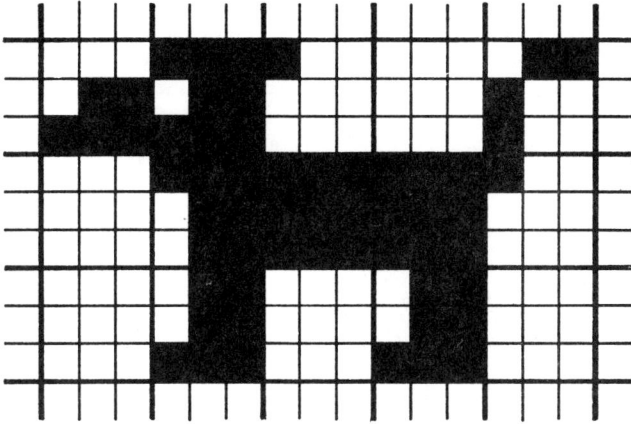

Figure 20.1   Dog design for Project 1.

READING THE KEYBOARD

At the moment, the only way we can send the Oric messages is via an INPUT command, which stops any screen activity, prints out messages, and generally tramples all over the graphic display. There are two other commands that can be used for messageless inputs:

GET

KEY$

The GET command lets you input a character, thought of as a string variable of length 1. If you type, say.

GET F$

then the Oric will *wait* until a key is pressed, and give that value to the variable F$. Try this:

    10   GET F$

    20   PRINT "YOU PRESSED KEY▽"; F$

    30   GOTO 10

and press keys.

For most video-game programs, GET isn't the command you want, because of the wait. Instead, you use KEY$. The syntax is slightly different: what corresponds to GET F$ above is:

F$ = KEY$

This sets F$ to the character being pressed, if there is one; and sets it to the *empty* string " " if not. It does *not* wait. In other words, KEY$ lets you read the keyboard to see which key, if any, is currently being pressed. You can then act on that information, as in the next section.

CYRIL THE SQUIRREL

(Or, for Americans, SHIRL THE SQUIRL.) Cyril the squirrel is sitting under a tree when nuts start falling around him. He rushes off to collect them, but they keep on coming: can Cyril collect them all? Your job is to make Cyril chase round the screen. The program gets a good bit longer than any I've given you before, and even then it could be improved; but it will teach you several useful techniques.

Figure 20.2 shows Cyril and a nut. In the alternate character set, Cyril is "NN =" and the nut is "(". The four arrow keys at the bottom of the keyboard move Cyril in the corresponding directions. The REM statements are there to remind me what I was doing: I've put them at funny line numbers so that you can omit them without affecting GOTOs.

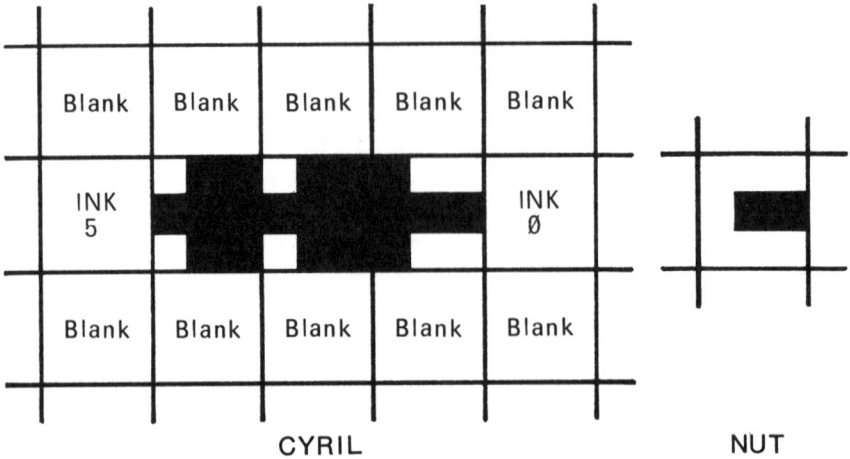

Figure 20.2 Cyril the Squirrel and a Nut. Note Cyril's border, and his attributes placed within it.

```
  9  REM INITIALIZE
 10  PRINT CHR$(6)
 20  CLS
 30  LORES1
 40  INK 3
 50  C = 18:R = 12:T = 8

 99  REM COLUMN OF NUTS
100  FOR Q = 8 TO 15
110  PLOT 6, Q, "("
120  NEXT Q

199  REM DISPLAY CYRIL
200  PLOT C, R − 1, "▽▽▽▽▽"
210  PLOT C, R, CHR$(5) + "NN = " + CHR$(3)
220  PLOT C, R + 1, "▽▽▽▽▽"

299  REM RANDOM NUT
300  IF RND(1) < .95 THEN 400
310  NR = 3 + 20 * RND(1)
320  NC = 5 + 30 * RND(1)
330  PLOT NC, NR, "("
340  T = T + 1
```

```
399   REM KEYBOARD SCAN
400   A$ = KEY$
410   IF A$ = " " THEN 600
420   A = ASC(A$)
430   IF A = 8 THEN C = C − 1
440   IF A = 9 THEN C = C + 1
450   IF A = 10 THEN R = R + 1
460   IF A = 11 THEN R = R − 1
470   IF R < 1 THEN R = 1
480   IF R > 25 THEN R = 25
490   IF C < 2 THEN C = 2
500   IF C > 32 THEN C = 32

599   REM SEARCH FOR NUTS
600   FOR E = 0 TO 4
610   FOR F = − 1 TO 1
620   IF SCRN(C + E, R + F) = 40 THEN ZAP: T = T − 1
630   NEXT F
640   NEXT E

699   REM CHECK NUT TOTAL
700   IF T > 0 THEN 200
710   PLOT 1, 1, CHR$(8) + CHR$(17) + "WELL DONE CYRIL!"
720   PRINT CHR$(6)
730   INK 0
740   STOP
```

Now for the low-down . . .

Line 10 turns off the keyboard bleep; 20–40 go into LORES1 and set yellow ink. In line 50, C and R are the positions directly ahead of Cyril's nose; and T is the total number of nuts on screen.

Lines 100–120 set up eight nuts, to avoid the game being over before it's begun.

Lines 200–220 plot Cyril. He has an 'invisible border' all round (for motion in all four directions, like the goat's invisible tail but better). Two characters in the border are ink attributes, the characters CHR$(5) and CHR$(0) in line 210. See Figure 20.2. These make Cyril purple, but don't affect the rest of the screen.

Lines 300–340 set up a random nut. If you drop a nut on *every* run through the program sequence, poor old Cyril soon gets buried: he just can't keep up. So line 300 gives a one-in-twenty chance of dropping a nut. This is about right; but for an easier game change the .95 to about .97; for a much harder one, to .9. Recall that "(" is the nut.

Lines 400 onwards are the main item to understand. They scan the keyboard looking for arrow key-presses. The ASCII codes for the arrow keys are like this:

← has ASCII code 8
→ has ASCII code 9
↓ has ASCII code 10
↑ has ASCII code 11

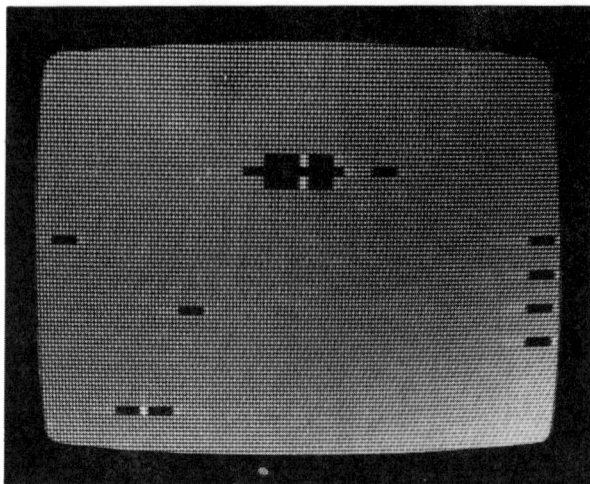

Figure 20.3 Cyril and some nuts as seen on TV.

Line 410 jumps if no key is pressed (to avoid a crash in line 420); lines 430–460 adjust the position of Cyril's nose according to the arrows. Lines 470–500 protect against going off screen: when Cyril hits an edge, he waits until you send him back towards the centre.

Lines 600 onwards search for a nut. When Cyril or his invisible border lands on a nut, the nut disappears from the screen display; but the computer can only realize this—and change the nut total T accordingly—if we search through the area occupied by Cyril and his border (Figure 20.2 shows this to be a 3 × 5 rectangle) looking for nuts. This is where the command:

SCRN(C, R)

comes in handy. It gives the ASCII code of the screen character in column C, row R. The nut is "(" and has ASCII code 40, hence line 620. Did you know squirrels carry lasers?

Finally line 700 tests whether all nuts are gone. If not, the program goes back to line 200 to print Cyril in his new position. If they are, you get a message. The CHR$(8) produces printout in the *standard* character set. (See the *Manual* page 36.) CHR$(17) gives red paper. Line 720 turns the keyboard bleep back on, 730 resets black ink. These are just for tidiness. (Incidentally, if you BREAK the program, press CTRL/F to get the bleep back. Otherwise it comes back next time you run Cyril.)

ANSWER

Project 1

The rows of the dog are characters numbered:

88	91	33	32	54
32	75	95	95	33
32	90	32	90	32

Corresponding to characters:

X	[	!	▽	6
▽	K	£	£	!
▽	Z	▽	Z	▽

100

so we get:

```
10  CLS
20  LORES1
30  INK 4
40  FOR C = 30 TO 1 STEP −1
50  PLOT C, 10, "X[!∇6∇"
60  PLOT C, 11, "∇K££!∇"
70  PLOT C, 12, "∇Z∇Z∇∇"
80  NEXT C
90  GOTO 90
```

Note that the invisible tail is now at the right-hand end: not because the dog's facing the other way, but because he's *moving* the other way.

*Computer programs often require lists
of information: numbers or words. Many
games programs use lists of numbers to
control the positions of objects on the
screen. These lists are called:*

21 Arrays

An *array* is essentially a numbered list of items, like a laundry list:

1. Socks.
2. Shirt.
3. Pillowcase.
4. Pullover.

If someone wants item number 3, (s)he can look it up on the list to see what it is (here a pillowcase). There are two kinds of arrays: *numeric* arrays and *string* arrays. The rules for array names are just the same as for variable names. Suppose we want to store in the computer a list of the twelve months of the year, in order. Since month-names are strings, we need a string array, which we'll call MTH$. (What's wrong with using MONTH$?)

First, we must tell the computer *how long the list will be.* This is known as 'dimensioning the array' and it is done with a:

DIM

command, like this:

10   DIM MTH$(12)

Strictly speaking, you could get away with 11 instead of 12 because (for reasons I won't go into here) arrays in the Oric are numbered from 0: an array dimensioned to 12 as above has entries numbered 0, 1, 2, 3, 4, 5, 6, 7, 8, 9, 10, 11, 12—thirteen altogether! The simplest way to avoid getting confused is to ignore the 0 entry.

Next you need to tell the computer what the 12 entries are:

20   MTH$(1) = "JANUARY"

30   MTH$(2) = "FEBRUARY"

. . .

130   MTH$(12) = "DECEMBER"

I've used dots, but *you* will have to type all twelve months. Hard luck. You can now refer to any given entry in the array by using the name of the array, followed by the item number in brackets. For example:

MTH$(7)

turns out to be 'JULY', and so on.

So, to print out a given month, you could add the lines:

140   INPUT "NUMBER OF MONTH"; N

150   PRINT MTH$(N)

Similarly, you might want to tell the computer how many days each month has. You'd set up a numeric array, say MTHLGTH, using:

    10   DIM MTHLGTH(12)

and then assign values:

    20   MTHLGTH(1) = 31

    30   MTHLGTH(2) = 28

    40   MTHLGTH(3) = 31

         . . .

    130 MTHLGTH(12) = 31

If any array contains 11 or fewer 'slots' for entries, including the zero slot, it is not strictly necessary to dimension it beforehand. That is,

    DIM ARRAY (N)

is only needed for N bigger than 10. As always, it's good practice to dimension a smaller array regardless, for clarity.

The Frequency Chart program in Chapter 15 used an array C of size 6. I cheated there, and didn't dimension it, because I didn't want to have to explain the DIM command at that stage. Go back and take a look at the way the array is used.

THE MOVING ZIT REVISITED

You may recall that in Chapter 9 I constructed a sort of 'delay line' to produce a moving worm. I used a whole list of variables C0, C1, . . . , C6 and R1, R2, . . . , R6 (in Project 4). As they stand, these do not form an array: the brackets are missing and as far as Oric is concerned, I might as well have called them SLEEPY, HAPPY, GRUMPY, BASHFUL and so on. Specifically, if I tried to refer to a general one of them by using CN, expecting to get C3 if N = 3, or C5 if N = 5, I'd be in for a nasty shock. Oric would look for a variable named:

    CN

fail to find it, and set it to zero by default. If however I'd put brackets in, and asked for:

    C(N)

it would check what value N had, say 5, and work out C(5). So the answer to Project 4 of Chapter 9 would become:

    41 FOR N = 0 TO 5

    42 C(N) = C(N + 1): R(N) = R(N + 1)

    43 NEXT N

    44 C(6) = C: R(6) = R

It would also be a good idea to dimension the two arrays:

    15 DIM C(6)

    16 DIM R(6)

and this could actually be shortened to:

    15 DIM C(6), R(6)

Project 1

Modify the size of the arrays C and R, and the loop size, to produce a worm of length 17. (Now you *must* dimension C and R beforehand!)

MULTIDIMENSIONAL ARRAYS

So far my arrays have only required one entry N to specify which item I want: the array is just a *list*. If I want a rectangular *table* of numbers or strings, I can use an array like this:

ARRAY(M, N)

This is called a two-dimensional array, because it needs two numbers. You can think of the entries as being arranged like this:

ARRAY(0, 0)	ARRAY(0, 1)	...	ARRAY(0, Y)
ARRAY(1, 0)	ARRAY(1, 1)	...	ARRAY(1, Y)
ARRAY(2, 0)	ARRAY(2, 1)	...	ARRAY(2, Y)
...	...	...	...
ARRAY(X, 0)	ARRAY(X, 1)	...	ARRAY(X, Y)

which is set up by the command (which is *never* optional for two or more dimensions):

DIM ARRAY(X, Y)

with specific numbers for X and Y. As before, entries with values 0 come as a bonus: I've separated them off by a dotted line. To avoid confusion, they can be ignored if they're not useful. So, to represent an 8 × 8 chessboard, you would use something like:

DIM CHESS(8, 8)

and enter numerical codes for the various pieces on each square.

For an example of the use of a two-dimensional array, see the Character Builder program in Chapter 28.

There are also three-dimensional arrays (and higher!) using:

DIM(X, Y, Z, . . .)

but they're rarely useful—and eat up memory wholesale.

ANSWER

Project 1

```
15   DIM C(16), R(16)
41   FOR N = 0 TO 15
42   C(N) = C(N + 1): R(N) = R(N + 1)
43   NEXT N
44   C(16) = C: R(16) = R
```

(Plus the lines of the original program.)

Music hath charms . . .
Here's my contribution to the
Bach-to-BASIC movement.

22 Music and Harmony

One of the nicest things about the Oric is its sophisticated sound chip. So far we've only used it to generate the standard games noises—ZAP, EXPLODE and so on. Now we should explore its capabilities somewhat further, and use it to play some music. When you write:

    100   ZAP:ZAP

the Oric is actually doing quite a lot of work for you in forming the right sound, or more precisely, combinations of sounds. In principle, it would be possible to extend this approach into music and have statements such as:

    200   BEETHOVENS 5TH

and expect a whole symphony to be played. But *huge* amounts of memory would be involved, and while it might be possible to store a few tunes in the machine, it would obviously be much more sensible to allow the user to specify a melody in terms of what instruments are playing which notes at what times and for how long.

Put another way, we want the Oric to respond to a set of instructions in much the same way as an orchestra responds to a piece of sheet music. And that's (almost) what the sound chip can be made to do.

MUSIC

The 'orchestra' is a little primitive, though. First, it has at most three musicians. (The Oric calls them tone channels.) Second, all of them have to play the same instrument! The distinction between different musical instruments is that, although they may be playing the same note, the quality of the sound varies in a number of ways. In practice, for instance, the number and volume of the harmonics in the note are characteristic of the instrument producing it. The Oric does not (directly) allow you to take account of this. However, a second feature is the way in which the volume of the note changes throughout its length. For instance, a guitar note starts loudly and gradually dies away; a violin has a more or less continuous volume, because the string is being continuously vibrated by the bow; the sound in an organ pipe builds up as it fills with air.

The Oric does allow us to mimic these features by specifying the *envelope* of the sound to be generated. The diagram at the bottom of page 100 of the *Manual* shows the possible envelopes, and for the above examples you can see that a guitar is equivalent to envelope mode 1, a violin might be mode 7 and an organ, mode 2. Don't expect the notes to sound *too* lifelike—you have to use a little imagination.

Now to play something. There are two commands needed—MUSIC and PLAY. For a rough analogy, MUSIC is equivalent to the musician looking at his sheet music to decide what note to play, and PLAY is equivalent to the conductor saying when it should be played.

So a MUSIC command needs to specify which musician (or tone channel) it refers to, which note is to be played, and how loud the note is to be. The note to be played is actually split into two parts; the octave (0–6) and the note within the octave. The note is evaluated like this:

Music Symbols	C	C# / Db	D	D# / Eb	E	F	F# / Gb	G	G# / Ab	A	A# / Bb	B
Oric Value	1	2	3	4	5	6	7	8	9	10	11	12

Note that C# is the same as Db, D# is the same as Eb etc. There is no E# or B#.

So suppose we want a middle C played by musician 2. We write:

```
20   MUSIC 2,   3,   1,   0
```
- Volume level
- Note 1(C)
- Octave (the middle one)
- Channel (musician) number

Notice that I've set the volume level to zero, which looks odd, because you might expect that to mean 'noiseless' or at least 'very quiet'. I'll explain its actual significance later.

Now for the conductor's bit. He has to say which musician is to play and what he's to sound like:

```
30   PLAY 2,   0,   1,   2000
```
- Time envelope lasts
- Envelope mode 1 (guitar)
- Always zero for our purposes
- Channel 2 on

RUN this. You'll hear a somewhat guitar-like note. Now experiment a little. Change the envelope length from 2000 to 20 000. It lasts too long for a guitar note, doesn't it? And 200 gives far too clipped a sound. Very roughly, for every 1000, you get 1 second, but the subjective effect is for the time to appear shorter than that, because it dies to a volume below the ear's threshold before it actually disappears.

Now try envelope mode 4. We can hear the envelope shape all right, but why doesn't it stop? Well, we haven't told it to. For envelope modes 1 and 2 there's an implied length in the final value of the PLAY instruction; but this is ignored by the 'continuous' modes 3–7. So now we need a way to stop the sound once it's started.

Obviously, we need to turn off the tone channels. So another PLAY instruction should follow line 30 which will do this:

```
40   PLAY 0, 0, 0, 0
```

should do.

RUN again. Now the sound has gone completely except for a hardly discernible click. The sound has been turned on at line 30 all right, but it's then immediately turned off at line 40! We need a delay between the two:

35   WAIT 200

which should give about 2 seconds of sound. And it does!

Now change the Ø (for volume level) in line 2Ø to 6. The note now has a fixed volume. So putting a value other than Ø in this position overrides the envelope shape in the subsequent PLAY command. And Ø doesn't mean 'zero volume': it means 'use the envelope to control the volume'.

In principle, that's all there is to using the tone channels, but, obviously, we need an easy way of getting the right note values and WAIT lengths into a program containing MUSIC commands. There are a number of possibilities for this, but one of the simplest involves using READ and DATA statements, as in Chapter 7.

So now to our program. For every note played, we need three pieces of information: the octave, the note and its length.

10   READ NTE, OCT, L

(Careful! You can't call a variable 'NOTE' because it includes the keyword 'NOT'.)

Now we want to play it:

20   MUSIC 2, OCT, NTE, Ø   (Output to channel 2)

25   PLAY 2, Ø, 2, 2200   (Open channel 2 with envelope 2
                                   lasting around 2 seconds)

then wait for a bit:

30   WAIT 20 * L

and get the next note:

35   GOTO 10

We've created the dreaded endless loop, though, so we need a delimiter of some sort. Suppose the last note to be played is given a length of zero. Then we could insert:

15   IF L = Ø THEN PLAY Ø, Ø, Ø, Ø:END

Now all that's needed is a DATA list for the READ to get its numbers from. Try this:

    50   DATA 1, 3, 2
    60   DATA 5, 3, 2
    70   DATA 5, 3, 2
    80   DATA 3, 3, 2
    90   DATA 1, 3, 2
   100   DATA 6, 3, 2
   110   DATA 6, 3, 2
   120   DATA 5, 3, 2
   130   DATA 3, 3, 2
   140   DATA 5, 3, 2
   150   DATA 8, 3, 2
   160   DATA 8, 3, 2
   170   DATA 7, 3, 2
   180   DATA 8, 3, 4
   190   DATA 5, 3, 2
   200   DATA 10, 3, 3
   210   DATA 8, 3, 1

```
220   DATA 6, 3, 2
230   DATA 5, 3, 2
240   DATA 3, 3, 2
250   DATA 1, 3, 2
260   DATA 12, 2, 2
270   DATA 5, 3, 2
280   DATA 3, 3, 2
290   DATA 1, 3, 2
300   DATA 1, 3, 2
310   DATA 12, 2, 2
320   DATA 1, 3, 4
600   DATA 0, 0, 0
```

Maybe that's topical if you had your Oric as a Christmas present!

But my real reason for choosing it is that most of the notes are the same length and in the same octave, making it easy to work out. You'll see that each DATA statement represents one note, in the order 'note, octave, length' as you'd expect, since that's the order READ wants them in. For instance:

```
170   DATA 7, 3, 2
```

specifies F# in octave 3 played for a length 2. I've chosen 2 as a standard length for a crotchet (so 1 will be a quaver) and, for two reasons, I've then multiplied this by 20 in the WAIT statement (line 30) to give the actual delay. First, it's easier to think 1s, 2s and 3s when writing the DATA statements. Second, you can alter the tempo simply by changing the 20 in line 30. You could even input a tempo value at the start.

I could have worked out the values for each DATA statement by looking at the sheet music for 'While Shepherds Watched' (Oh, so *that's* what it was!), but in fact I did it by ear and guesswork. (What do you mean, you can tell?) That's why the delimiting statement is at 600. I put it in first, so that I could repeatedly run the program as I inserted new DATA statements, to check each additional one. 600 was just a guess at a line number which would not be likely to be reached.

Project 1

Using the same program, modify the DATA statements to play 'Don't Cry for Me, Argentina'.

HARMONY

The Oric's sound chip is actually a lot cleverer than the previous example gives it credit for. Try this (I'll explain how it works after you've been suitably impressed):

```
 5   CH = 2
10   READ NTE, OCT, L, N2, O2
15   IF L = 0 THEN PLAY 0,0,0,0:RESTORE:WAIT 50: CH = 5 – CH: GOTO 10
20   MUSIC 2, OCT, NTE, 7  ⎤
                            ⎬ Change 7 to 4 for lower volume if you wish.
22   MUSIC 1, O2 – 1, N2, 7 ⎦
25   PLAY CH, 0, 0, 0
30   WAIT 20 * L
35   GOTO 10
```

```
40   DATA 5, 3, 1, 5, 3
50   DATA 1, 3, 1, 5, 3
60   DATA 3, 3, 1, 5, 3
70   DATA 5, 3, 1, 5, 3
80   DATA 8, 3, 1, 5, 3
90   DATA 6, 3, 1, 5, 3
100  DATA 6, 3, 1, 6, 3
110  DATA 10, 3, 1, 6, 3
120  DATA 8, 3, 1, 6, 3
130  DATA 8, 3, 1, 8, 3
140  DATA 1, 4, 1, 8, 3
150  DATA 12, 3, 1, 8, 3
160  DATA 1, 4, 1, 8, 3
170  DATA 8, 3, 1, 8, 3
180  DATA 5, 3, 1, 8, 3
190  DATA 1, 3, 1, 6, 3
200  DATA 3, 3, 1, 6, 3
210  DATA 5, 3, 1, 6, 3
220  DATA 6, 3, 1, 5, 3
230  DATA 8, 3, 1, 5, 3
240  DATA 10, 3, 1, 5, 3
250  DATA 8, 3, 1, 5, 3
260  DATA 6, 3, 1, 5, 3
270  DATA 5, 3, 1, 5, 3
280  DATA 3, 3, 1, 1, 3
290  DATA 5, 3, 1, 1, 3
300  DATA 1, 3, 1, 1, 3
310  DATA 12, 2, 1, 12, 2
320  DATA 1, 3, 1, 12, 2
330  DATA 3, 3, 1, 12, 2
340  DATA 8, 2, 1, 12, 2
350  DATA 12, 2, 1, 12, 2
360  DATA 3, 3, 1, 12, 2
370  DATA 6, 3, 1, 12, 2
380  DATA 5, 3, 1, 12, 2
390  DATA 3, 3, 1, 12, 2
400  DATA 5, 3, 1, 5, 3
410  DATA 1, 3, 1, 5, 3
420  DATA 3, 3, 1, 5, 3
430  DATA 5, 3, 1, 5, 3
```

```
440   DATA 8, 3, 1, 5, 3
450   DATA 6, 3, 1, 5, 3
460   DATA 6, 3, 1, 6, 3
470   DATA 10, 3, 1, 6, 3
480   DATA 8, 3, 1, 6, 3
490   DATA 8, 3, 1, 8, 3
500   DATA 1, 4, 1, 8, 3
510   DATA 12, 3, 1, 8, 3
520   DATA 1, 4, 1, 8, 3
530   DATA 8, 3, 1, 8, 3
540   DATA 5, 3, 1, 8, 3
550   DATA 1, 3, 1, 6, 3
560   DATA 3, 3. 1, 6, 3
570   DATA 5, 3, 1, 6, 3
580   DATA 10, 2, 1, 5, 3
590   DATA 8, 3, 1, 5, 3
600   DATA 6, 3, 1, 5, 3
610   DATA 5, 3, 1, 5, 3
620   DATA 3, 3, 1, 5, 3
630   DATA 1, 3, 1, 5, 3
640   DATA 8, 2, 1, 12, 2
650   DATA 1, 3, 1, 12, 2
660   DATA 12, 2, 1, 12, 2
670   DATA 1, 3, 6, 1, 3
1000  DATA 0, 0, 0, 0, 0
```

If you've been careful, and got all the DATA statements right, you should hear Bach's 'Jesu, Joy of Man's Desiring', played alternately without and with a harmony line. Sounds good, doesn't it?

Now, how does it work? Well, in some respects it's pretty similar to the previous program, except that now we're giving instructions to two 'musicians' instead of just one. So each DATA statement now has five values associated with it. The first three are as before (note, octave, length). The last two are note and octave values for the second musician (channel). We don't need a second length value, because the harmony line happens to be related very simply (in this case) to the melody.

You'll notice that there's an additional line 22 which outputs the harmony line to channel 1 (N2 and O2 having been picked up in the READ statement). Note that the octave selected for the harmony is one below the melody (O2 − 1), to give some 'spread' to the sound. Of course, I could have allowed for this in the DATA statements, but I'd written a lot of them before I realized I needed to do this, so it was easier just to subtract one in the appropriate MUSIC statement.

Now to PLAY the MUSIC that's been set up in lines 20 and 22:

25   PLAY CH, 0, 0, 0

We're not using an envelope (because the volume is set to 7 in both MUSIC commands) so only the channel needs to be defined in PLAY. Hence the last three zeros. CH is initialized to 2 (line 5) which means that only channel 2 will be open. So although channel 1 is set up ready to play a note, it can't because PLAY won't let it. As a result, first time round there's no harmony.

However, when the program reaches the delimiting data in line 1000, L is zero, and the condition in line 15 is met. Before restarting, CH is set to 5 − CH. Since CH is 2 at the moment, it will become 3, and CH = 3 opens channels 1 and 2! Next time CH will be 5 − 3 = 2 and the harmony is turned off again, etc. etc., ad infinitum. See page 100 of the *Manual* under the heading 'Tone enable' for the effects of setting CH in the range 0–7.

Looking back on this, it's clear that the program is trivial, and then there are piles of DATA statements. Couldn't we reduce the requirement for repetitive data by making the program more complex? Well, yes, but I wanted to get an impressive result without having to spend pages discussing an appropriate data structure and ways of handling it. There simply isn't space for that.

But I ought to give you some ideas to work on. The general problem is that we may have a melody line which looks something like this:

C	G	F	G	G	A	. . .

and a harmony like this:

D	D				F	. . .

In other words the harmony notes do not have to be the *same* multiples of the basic beat time. (In 'Jesu, Joy of Man's Desiring' they are; that's what makes it an easy example).

Now, to take the above example, it means we have to send channel information as well as note and octave (and volume if we want crescendos and pianissimos). Considering just note and channel:

Note		Channel(s)	Channel code
Ch1	Ch2		
C	D	1 + 2	3
G	D	1 + 2	3
F	D*	1	1
G	D*	1	1
G	D*	1	1
A	F	1 + 2	3

The starred notes could actually be anything because they aren't played. We need to put them in if we continue to adopt a system in which every set of data has a fixed number of items. We don't *have* to do this, although if we don't, it becomes necessary to read one item at a time, checking for appropriate delimiters as we go. This may make the processing longer for some notes than others, and so mess up the rhythm.

ANSWER

Project 1

The DATA lines you need are:

    50   DATA 7, 3, 4

    60   DATA 7, 3, 2

    70   DATA 7, 3, 2

    80   DATA 7, 3, 4

```
 90  DATA 8, 3, 2
100  DATA 10, 3, 2
110  DATA 12, 3, 2
120  DATA 10, 3, 2
130  DATA 10, 3, 2
140  DATA 12, 3, 4
150  DATA 12, 3, 2
160  DATA 10, 3, 2
170  DATA 3, 4, 6
180  DATA 10, 3, 2
190  DATA 8, 3, 4
200  DATA 7, 3, 4
210  DATA 7, 3, 3
220  DATA 8, 3, 3
230  DATA 10, 3, 2
240  DATA 5, 3, 8
250  DATA 5, 3, 3
260  DATA 7, 3, 3
270  DATA 8, 3, 2
280  DATA 3, 3, 10
290  DATA 3, 3, 2
300  DATA 5, 3, 2
310  DATA 3, 3, 2
320  DATA 7, 3, 4
330  DATA 10, 3, 6
340  DATA 10, 2, 2
350  DATA 10, 2, 2
360  DATA 10, 2, 2
370  DATA 12, 2, 4
380  DATA 3, 3, 6
600  DATA 0, 0, 0
```

Of course, you'll get different values if you used a different musical key.

*How to get the computer to debug
itself!*

23 Debugging IV

In Chapter 18 I talked about *dry-running* a program, to trace by hand the flow of commands. The main flaw in this technique is that the user—you—must do all the work: the Oric just sits there smugly telling you it has no idea what you're talking about, or worse still, gives all the wrong answers. It's time to make it work for its living.

It can be made to generate its own dry-run tables. Take the program used as an example in Chapter 18, for instance. It's supposed to find the maximum and minimum of a series of inputs. But it doesn't! Here's how to find out where the error(s) are. Add a line 5, to print out the table headings, and then on every line, print the line number and any value which is altered on that line, in the appropriate columns:

```
5   PRINT "LN∇∇∇MAX∇∇MIN∇∇N∇∇∇∇BRANCH"
10  MAX = 0: MIN = 0: PRINT "10"; TAB(5); MAX; TAB(10); MIN
20  INPUT N: PRINT "20"; TAB(15); N
30  IF N < MIN THEN MIN = N: PRINT "30"; TAB(10); MIN
40  IF N > MAX THEN MAX = N: PRINT "40"; TAB(5); MAX
50  IF N < 0 THEN PRINT MAX, MIN: END
60  PRINT "60"; TAB(20); "V": GOTO 20
```

The TAB command just produces printing in the corresponding screen column. The form of the resulting table is slightly different from the hand produced one. Lines on which no alterations occur are not listed but, if anything, that makes it easier to follow. A more serious problem is that the input prompts and values break the table up. If you've got a printer, it's easy to get over this one—just replace each PRINT with LPRINT and the table will appear on the printer. In any case, it's better to have printed output to study because the chances are the table will occupy more than a screenful.

If you haven't got a printer, you may wish to economize on the number of values printed. For instance, in this case, simply knowing the values in MAX and MIN at the end of every loop will probably be enough. So it would be adequate just to add a line 55 to the original program:

55   PRINT MAX, MIN

You may want to change the variables to examine on different test runs. A neat trick is to edit a REM into a PRINT statement you want to deactivate, like this:

55   REM PRINT MAX, MIN

Since line 55 is now a comment, the computer will ignore it. If you want it back later, this saves you retyping the line—just edit out the REM.

So the Oric can tell us how its variables are changing. There are two other useful things it could do:

1. It could tell us which lines it executes, and in which order.
2. It could tell us how often it executes particular lines or blocks of code.

TRACES

The first of these features is built into BASIC. There are two commands. TRON (nothing to do with Walt Disney—it's short for TRace ON) and TROFF (TRace OFF).

Try typing TRON:RUN as a direct command, with a program already in memory. You'll see the line numbers, enclosed in square brackets, appear on the screen as the lines are executed. (The *Manual* says that TRON can't be used in immediate mode, which is true; but it will work that way if followed by RUN as part of *a single multistatement command.*)

Traces can be more confusing than useful if they are used with gay abandon. With any debugging procedure you must be careful to ask sensible questions, and then get the machine to provide the answers to *just* those questions. There's no point in doing a complete dry run if all you want to know is whether a particular variable ever gets to 25. The more data you ask the machine to print, the longer it will take you to analyse it. So it is with traces. If you are sure that a particular block of code is executing correctly, why bother to trace it? In other words, you should use TRON and TROFF as *program* statements to turn the trace on and off while the program is running. By and large, we'll be concerned to trace a program in the vicinity of branches.

Here's an example. We write a piece of code which accepts a day of the month for use elsewhere in a program. It's good practice to test the value entered to ensure that it's in the range 1–31. We *could* do more sophisticated tests to check that the value isn't greater than 29 if the month is February and so on, but we'll stick to the simplest checks here.

Our first attempt might be:

```
50   INPUT "ENTER DAY OF MONTH"; D

60   IF D > 0 OR D < 32 THEN 200

70   PRINT "NOT A POSSIBLE DAY"

80   GOTO 50

        . . .

200   REM HERE FOR A VALID DAY
```

The program doesn't behave correctly, so we could insert:

```
45    TRON

90    TROFF

205   TROFF
```

and edit 200:

```
200   TRON: REM HERE FOR A VALID DAY
```

to trace just the code under suspicion. (Be careful not to insert a line 195   TRON—it would never be executed because of the . . . THEN 200 on line 60.)

When this is run we find that, regardless of what value is entered for D, the trace always shows up as:

```
[50] [60] [200] [205]
```

Line 70 cannot be reached. Line 60 *should* have read:

```
60   IF D > 0 AND D < 32 THEN 200
```

If you think about it, *any* number is either greater than 0 or less than 32!

114

This problem crops up fairly often, because we are rather careless in the way we use the words AND and OR in ordinary speech, and this carelessness can be transferred to our programming. Most of the time, in conversation, a listener has a fair idea what the speaker means, probably even before he has completed a sentence, so we can get away with little inexactitudes.

The Oric is much more pedantic.

PROGRAM PROFILES

A program profile shows how many times each line of a program has been executed. As usual, this is overkill, and we should be selective about the parts of a program we want to profile. It's easy enough to do. Suppose that we want to find out how many times line 420 of a particular program is executed. We set up a count to zero at the beginning of the program and then increment it by 1 every time line 420 is passed through:

```
 50   PC = 0

      . . .

420   A = A * (P − 1)
421   PC = PC + 1

      . . .

800   PRINT PC
810   STOP
```

Let's look at a concrete example. The following program is intended to accept a maximum of 20 values, terminated by zero, and sort them into ascending order. Thus if the input sequence is:

```
3
8
1
4
2
0
```

the resulting output should be:

```
1
2
3
4
8
```

The zero should not appear since it is only a delimiter.

```
10   DIM A(20)
20   FOR P = 1 TO 20
30   INPUT A(P)
40   IF A(P) = 0 THEN 60
50   NEXT P
60   N = P
```

```
 65   F = 0
 70   FOR P = 1 TO N
 80   IF A(P) < A(P + 1) THEN 130
 90   T = A(P)
100   A(P) = A(P + 1)
110   A(P + 1) = T
120   F = 1
130   NEXT P
140   IF F = 1 THEN 65
150   FOR P = 1 TO N
160   PRINT A(P)
170   NEXT P
```

The program doesn't quite do the job. (Key it in and try it.) In fact it gets into an endless loop.

So where to start looking? The first loop (20–50) looks harmless enough, and the final one (150–170) is just printing out the contents of the array, A. It seems sensible then to concentrate on the loop from 70 to 130. It is clear from line 80 that sometimes all the statements in the loop are executed, and sometimes those from 90 to 120 are ignored. So we'll have two profile counts, C1 and C2, which count the number of times the loop is entered and the number of times the last part of the loop is executed, respectively.

We can achieve this with:

```
 67   C1 = 0
 68   C2 = 0
 75   C1 = C1 + 1
125   C2 = C2 + 1
132   PRINT C1, C2
```

While we are at it, we might as well print out the contents of the array at the end of each loop because it is obvious that numbers are being shovelled about inside it and that very few other variables are being used at all. So:

```
134   FOR Q= 1 TO N          (because 1 to N seems to be the
135   PRINT A(Q);             relevant chunk of the array)
136   NEXT Q
137   PRINT
138   FOR X = 1 TO 200: NEXT X        (pause)
```

Let's try a few data sets and see what happens; if we enter:

```
3
6
1
8
5
0
```

we get:

```
6   4
316500
6   4
130056
6   2
100356
6   2
001356
6   2
001356
6   1
001356
6   1
001356
```

and so on, indefinitely.

Well, it seems to be getting values in order but we've lost the '8' and where did the pair of zeros come from? Also, it goes round the main loop 6 times consistently but the number of times round the subloop decreases steadily until it reaches 1, where it stays.

One of the zeros is obviously the delimiter, and the other one is an element of the array which is not set during the run, but is initialized to zero by the system. In other words, the program is dealing with two values too many. So let's rewrite line 60:

   60   $N = P - 2$

and try yet again. Hope beats eternal . . . We get:

```
4          2
3165
4          2
1356
4          0
1356
1
3
5
6
```

It's progress of a kind: we've got rid of those zeros. But we still haven't got our 8 back.

It's hard to see how it can have got lost. Perhaps it's still there, but not being printed out. Where do we PRINT it? Lines 150–170. The range 1 TO N must be too small. Let's increase it by 1:

   150   FOR $P = 1$ TO $N + 1$

And, of course, while we're at it, the trace in line 134 is presumably having the same problems. So let's fix that up too:

   134   FOR $Q = 1$ TO $N + 1$

Ho hum; once more unto the breach, dear friends, once more. . .
This time we get (for the same data):

    4   2
    31658
    4   2
    13568
    4   Ø
    13568
    1
    3
    5
    6
    8

Great! we've cracked it. It's doing the job perfectly. Or is it? Let's try:

    3
    5
    2
    1
    5
    Ø

This time we get:

    4   3
    32155
    4   3
    21355
    4   2
    12355
    4   1
    12355
    4   1
    12355
    4   1
    12355
    . . .
    etc.

It's getting the right answer, but it never comes out of the loop. We notice that C2 never gets down to zero in this case so it's a fair bet that this is what terminates the program.

What decides whether the program enters the subloop or not? Line 80:

80   IF A(P) < A(P + 1) THEN 130

The difference between the two data sets is that the second has two identical values in it. Since 5 is not less than 5 the subloop will be executed whenever the pair of 5s is encountered. That's why the program always goes round the subloop once. Perhaps the condition should be:

80   IF A(P) < = A(P + 1) THEN 130

This time everything works.

```
4    2
32155
4    2
21355
4    1
12355
4    0
12355
1
2
3
5
5
```

Now it works like a charm and we can take out the test lines.

I hope I have illustrated a couple of important points here. Firstly, we haven't needed to know exactly how the procedure works. If you've worked through this carefully, it's probably fairly clear by now; and a few dry runs would probably convince you that you understand it. (Dry runs are a good way of understanding how computer procedures work. I've often done a dozen or so on some obscure piece of code—someone else's, of course—before being really clear in my mind about what's going on.) Secondly, there is always a temptation to believe that when a program runs successfully for the first time, the job is done and there's time for a quick pint down the local. As we've seen, the job is *not* done, because there may be other sets of data for which the program fails; and anyway, the pub closed an hour and a half ago, if time goes as fast for you as it does for me when I'm writing code.

Every location in the Oric's memory has its own address label. Two commands let you see what's stored at a given address, and change it:

24 Peek and Poke

This chapter delves a little more deeply than the rest into the actual *way* the machine works. Ordinarily, in BASIC, the machine itself does most of the routine work for you; so you don't need to worry about awkward questions like 'whereabouts in memory does this stuff live?' But I'll need to use the POKE command to set colours in high-resolution graphics (Chapter 26), and that command is intimately bound up with the way information is held in memory. So this chapter may help you understand how the later POKEs work. If you find it confusing, skip to the next chapter and come back later.

MEMORY ORGANIZATION

Computer memory is extremely systematic. Each memory location is given a fixed number, its *address*. Each address contains a number between 0 and 255 (one character's worth of information). This number is actually stored in *binary*, as a string of 0s and 1s. See the *Manual*, page 60, for the gory details.

Numbers between 0 and 255 can be written using *eight* binary digits 0 or 1; for instance:

173 (decimal) = 10101101 (binary).

A string of eight binary digits, or *bits*, is called a *byte*. (There is a numbering system 'intermediate' between the two, called hexadecimal: see the *Manual* pages 60–63 if you're interested.)

The computer has two types of memory:

1. ROM (Read Only Memory) which contains its operating system, the instructions that make it work.
2. RAM (Random Access Memory) which stores the things that can be changed: the BASIC program, screen displays, scratchpad for calculations, and so on.

You can alter the contents of RAM, but not of ROM. So the *worst* you can do by mucking about in memory is get the machine into a state that requires a RESET: you can't mess up the operating system. This lets you experiment without having to worry about ill-effects on the machine: there are none!

The front end of ROM looks like Table 24.1. And there are a good many thousand more bytes of information tucked away inside the Oric. When the computer is working, all those 0s and 1s scurry around inside like ants (well, the 1s are ants and the 0s are non-ants) until they end up where you, the programmer (and the people who wrote the ROM program) have commanded. Doesn't it make you feel awed and humble, having life-or-death control over so many ants?

Table 24.1

Address	Contents	
	Binary	Decimal
49152	01001100	76
49153	01011001	89
49154	11101010	234
49155	01001100	76
49156	01110101	117
49157	11000100	196
49158	01000000	64
49159	11001001	201

PEEK

The command that lets you look inside a memory location and see what's there (but *not* change it) is:

PEEK

For instance, to find the contents of address 49153, enter:

PRINT PEEK 49153

You should see 89 appear: if not, I've lied to you.

The following program lets you PEEK any section of memory. It types out one screenful of information; if you hit a key, it will scroll up and give another screenful. This is called *paged* display, and is achieved by lines 70–80 of the program.

```
10  REM PEEKING ROUTINE          (don't omit this line!)
20  INPUT X
30  Y = PEEK(X)
40  PRINT X, Y,
50  IF Y > 31 AND Y < 128 OR Y > 159
    THEN PRINT CHR$(Y) ELSE PRINT "CTRL"
60  X = X + 1
70  K = K + 1
80  IF K = 25 THEN K = 0: GET A$
90  GOTO 30
```

RUN this and input 49152 for X: you should see the first 25 locations in ROM, and you can check the table above. (That's how I got it.) Press any key for the next page. Use CTRL/C *twice* to 'break' (the first is interpreted as the GET).

The actual numbers here don't seem to make much sense; nor should they: they're written in the Oric's private personal Machine Code (*Manual* page 123). It would take another book even to get you started on this. One thing you *will* realize, if you keep hitting a key for a new page, is that there's an awful lot of information filed away in ROM. And some of it, you'll even recognize.

Project 1

RUN the above program and input X = 49386; then again with X = 49836. What are you looking at?

NARCISSUS STRIKES AGAIN

Legend has it that Narcissus fell in love with his own reflection in a fountain and was turned into a flower (as an act of revenge by Artemis when Narcissus didn't fancy a nymph called Echo). Courting the same disaster, I'm going to make the PEEKing routine peek at itself!

Programs are stored in memory beginning at address 1280. If you RUN the routine on page 121 and input 1280 for X, this is what you get on the first page of display:

Address	Contents in decimal	Character
1280	0	CTRL
1281	23	CTRL
1282	5	CTRL
1283	10	CTRL
1284	0	CTRL
1285	157	CTRL
1286	32	(space)
1287	80	P
1288	69	E
1289	69	E
1290	75	K
1291	73	I
1292	78	N
1293	71	G
1294	32	(space)
1295	82	R
1296	79	O
1297	85	U
1298	84	T
1299	73	I
1300	78	N
1301	69	E
1302	0	CTRL
1303	31	CTRL
1304	5	CTRL

(The CTRL entries refer to control characters, some of which interfere with the screen synchronization, which is why the program includes line 50). I don't expect this to make total sense, but you can see the words PEEKING ROUTINE quite clearly. If you hit a key for a new page, you'll recognize other pieces of the program. The rest of the junk in the list either encodes the line numbers (in a less than transparent way) or the BASIC keywords, which are 'compressed' into a single code. (For instance the 157 in address 1285 stands for REM.) Yes folks: the program really *is* stored in the machine, and you can *see* it if you look in the right place.

Hmmmmm . . . nothing floral going on yet. Though I *am* starting to feel a little petunia . . . Maybe my secretary Cynthia can help. Hiya, Cynth!

POKE

Not only can you see the program: you can *change* it. Type in these direct commands:

POKE 1290, 86

POKE 1292, 83

POKE 1293, 72

Now LIST the program. The same? Not quite; doesn't the REM say:

PEEVISH ROUTINE

If you RUN the Peeking Tom routine again, you'll see what's happened: addresses 1290, 1292, and 1293 have had their contents changed to the codes for V, S, H instead of K, N, G. So the POKE command lets you insert a given byte into a memory location at a specified address.

Project 2

Change PEEKING ROUTINE into PARKING ROUTINE with two POKEs.

Now I've really opened Pandora's Box. If you can POKE memory locations at will, you can change anything you like—provided you know where it is. You can glean some information from the Memory Map in Appendix A of the *Manual*, assuming you can decipher what it's trying desperately to tell you. Two hints:

(a)   The addresses are given in Hex, for instance ROM starts at C000. To find this in decimal, use:

   PRINT #C000

   and the Oric will give you it in decimal, as 49152. Aha! so *that's* where he got it from . . .
(b)   If your Oric is a 16K version, not a 48K, subtract 32768 decimal from all addresses except those in ROM (at the top of the Map) and below 1280 (BOTH MODES at the bottom).

Project 3

What are the decimal values of the addresses for the start of:

(a)   The TEXT screen?
(b)   The HIRES screen?
(c)   The alternate character set in HIRES mode?
(d)   The standard character set in TEXT mode?

Anyway, you can have fun PEEKing all over the Memory Map; and if you feel like the odd POKE, by all means have a go. However, one warning: *random* POKEs seldom achieve much; you need to have some understanding of the system before you tinker with it, just like a motor car. Come to think of it, wasn't Pandora's Box full of *bugs*?

I IMAGINE HE PEEKED THE WRONG ADDRESS

Cosgrove   0-130

ANSWERS

Project 1

49386 gives the BASIC Keyword Table; 49836 gives the Error Message Table.

Project 2

POKE 1288, 65
POKE 1289, 82

Project 3

You'll need to look at the Memory Map in Appendix A of the *Manual*, and distinguish between HIRES and TEXT modes (left and right columns of the diagram). Now:

(a) **PRINT #BB80**   gives the address 48000 in decimal.
(b) **PRINT #A000**   gives the address 40960 in decimal.
(c) **PRINT #9C00**   gives the address 39936 in decimal.
(d) **PRINT #B400**   gives the address 46080 in decimal.

These are for the 48K machine: for the 16K subtract 32768 from each number, to get (a) 15232 (b) 8192 (c) 7168 (d) 13312.

Fine graphics on the Oric are just like coarse graphics, but use smaller blocks. Also there are several new features when you use:

25 High-resolution Graphics

This is where Oric really shows what it can do. In:

HIRES

mode (HIgh RESolution, nothing to do with rental services) it can draw pictures with much finer detail, often giving extremely beautiful results. If you need encouragement, thumb through the pictures in this chapter before reading on.

The High-resolution Screen is organized just like the Text Screen, as an array of cells, but each cell is much smaller. The rows go from 0 to 199, and the columns from 0 to 239, as in Figure 25.1. Note that both run from the top left corner. So altogether the screen can hold 200 * 240 = 48 000 cells! That's why it takes up so much memory—8160 bytes, in fact, or about *half* of the 16K memory. Each Text cell splits up into 48 Hi-res cells, as in Figure 25.2.

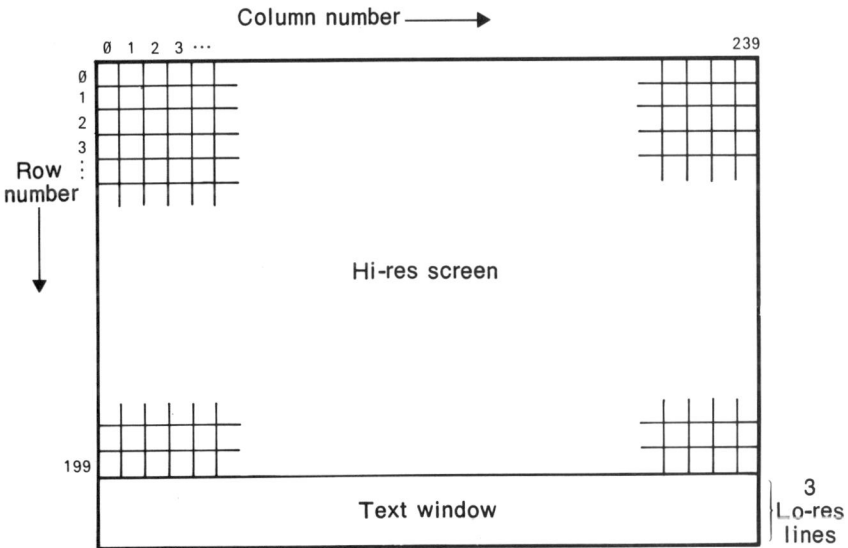

Figure 25.1   Structure of the Hi-res Screen for PLOT commands.

LINES

Key this program in and RUN it. It uses two new commands to produce straight lines:

CURSET

DRAW

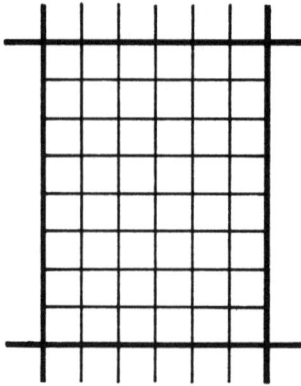

Figure 25.2   How a Lo-res cell divides into 48 Hi-res cells.

```
10   HIRES
20   FOR R = 5 TO 194 STEP 3
30   CURSET 5, R, 1
40   DRAW 228, 0, 1
50   NEXT R
60   FOR C = 5 TO 233 STEP 3
70   CURSET C, 5, 1
80   DRAW 0, 189, 1
90   NEXT C
```

Line 10 puts Oric into HIRES mode. (Note that a three-line Lo-res *Text Window* appears at the bottom of the screen—marvellous for inputs and immediate mode commands but useless for listing a program line because the 'Ready' message wipes it out.) Lines 20–50 rule lots of horizontal lines; lines 60–90 rule the vertical ones.

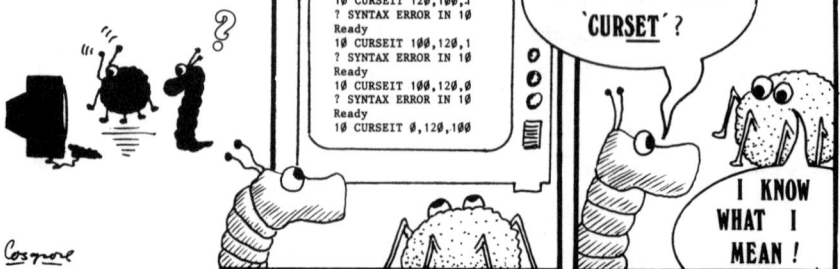

It works like this. The instruction:

CURSET C, R, K

sets the Hi-res cursor to column C (between 0 and 239), and row R (between 0 and 199). The third number, K, must be between 0 and 3. If K is 0 the cursor position is printed in PAPER colour (black unless you set it otherwise) so can't be seen; if K = 1 then the cursor is in INK colour and *can* be seen. (Ignore the other two values.) So:

CURSET 120, 100, 1

plots one Hi-res cell at 120, 100, which is the middle of the screen.

DRAW X, Y, K

now draws a straight line from the current cursor position C, R to the position that is *offset* by X columns and Y rows—that is, to C + X, R + Y as in Figure 25.3. Keep both ends on screen or you'll get an error message. The number K works as in CURSET, and to *see* the line, I suggest you always use DRAW X, Y, 1 until you get used to the way all these features work.

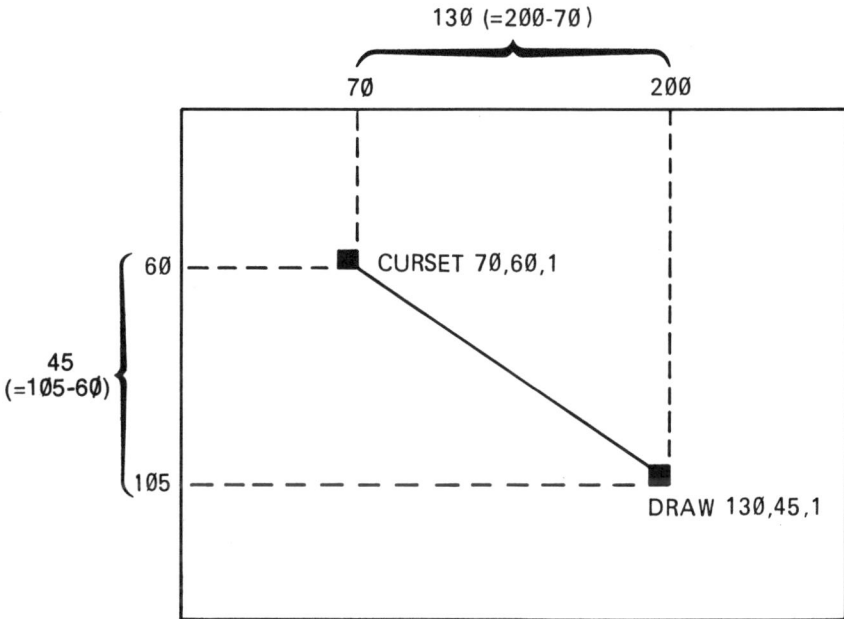

Figure 25.3   DRAW uses offset coordinates, not absolute.

There's also a command:

CURMOV X, Y, K

which offsets the cursor position by X and Y. So it has exactly the same effect as:

CURSET C + X, R + Y, K

where C, R is the current cursor position. However, offsets are often easier to work out, it depends.

To get out of Hi-res mode, use the direct command:

TEXT

Project 1

Use Figure 25.4 to write a HIRES program which draws two diamond shapes, one inside the other.

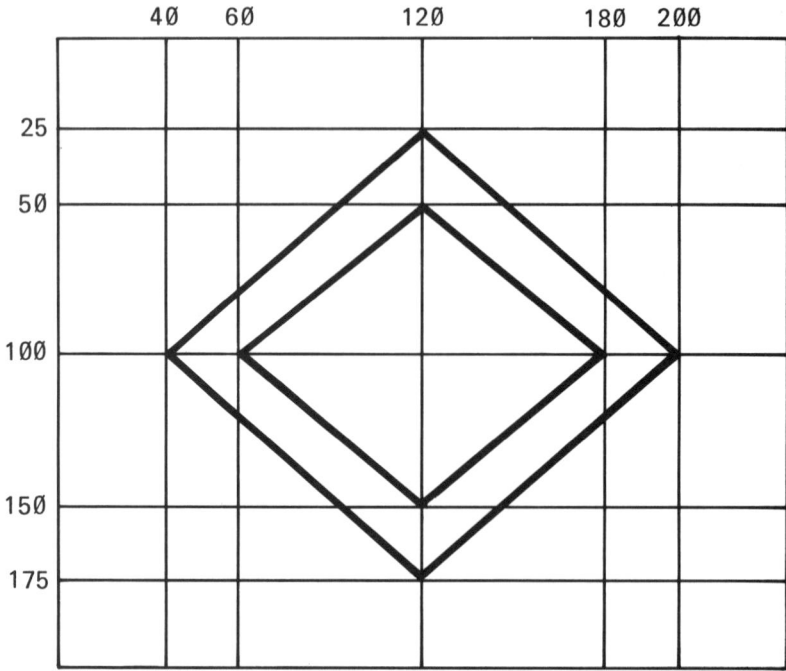

Figure 25.4   Diamond design for Project 1.

Here's something a bit fancier, to show that straight lines can be beautiful. Mathematicians call it an *envelope*.

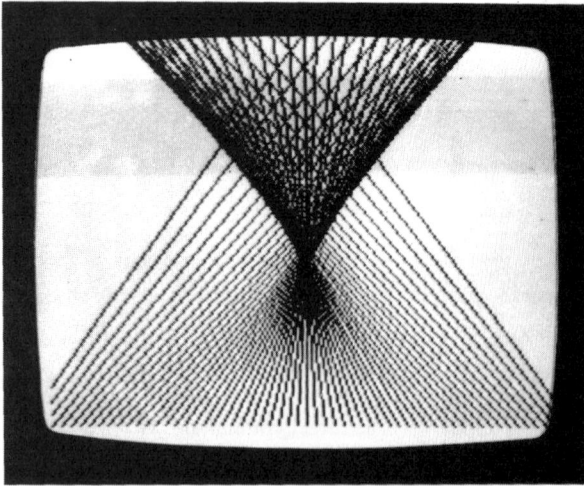

Figure 25.5   Envelope of a semicubical parabola formed from straight lines.

```
10  HIRES
20  INPUT S
30  FOR C = 0 TO 239 STEP S
40  CURSET C, 199, 1
50  X = C/120 − 1
60  X = X * X * X − X
70  DRAW 120 − C + 200 * X, − 199, 1
80  NEXT C
```

On the first run, input S = 3. Now try 1, 2, 4, 5, . . . as you wish. Most of the work goes into setting up formulas to give the endpoints of the lines.

When you've got one of these pictures on the Hi-res screen, see what happens if you use the direct commands:

PAPER 4

INK 6

and so on. You can also use INK and PAPER within HIRES mode as program commands. Hi-res colour is a bit tricky: see below for the gory but glorious details.

CIRCLES

The command:

CIRCLE W, 1

will draw in INK colour a circle, radius W, centred at the current Hi-res cursor position. W must be 1 or bigger. Similarly:

CIRCLE W, 0

will draw it in PAPER colour. (This isn't so silly: the second will *erase* the first, for example.) That means that drawing a circle really needs *two* steps, unless you're lucky:

1. Use CURSET or CURMOV to position the centre of the circle.
2. Use CIRCLE to draw it.

For instance, to draw a circle of radius 75 whose centre is at 120,100 you would use:

```
10  HIRES
20  CURSET 120, 100, 0
30  CIRCLE 75, 1
```

(The 0 at the end of line 20 prevents a central dot being plotted: change it to 1 and see what happens then.)

My Oric's circles look a little bit squashed: maybe Eric the nannygoat sat on them all. On more recent models they really do look *circular*.

Project 2

Draw ten concentric circles, centred at 150, 80 and of radii 5, 10, 15, . . . , 50.

SHOCKWAVES

When an aircraft flies, the atmospheric disturbance it causes spreads out in circular waves. But the circle moves with the aircraft. This program shows how supersonic flight produces a *shockwave* where the ripples overlap.

```
10  HIRES
20  FOR C = 5 TO 120 STEP 5
30  CURSET C + 20, 100, 0
40  CIRCLE C/2, 1
50  NEXT C
```

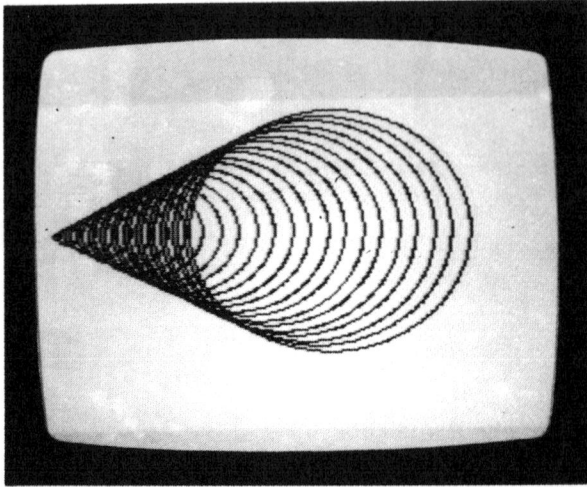

Figure 25.6   Supersonic wavefronts form a shockwave . . .

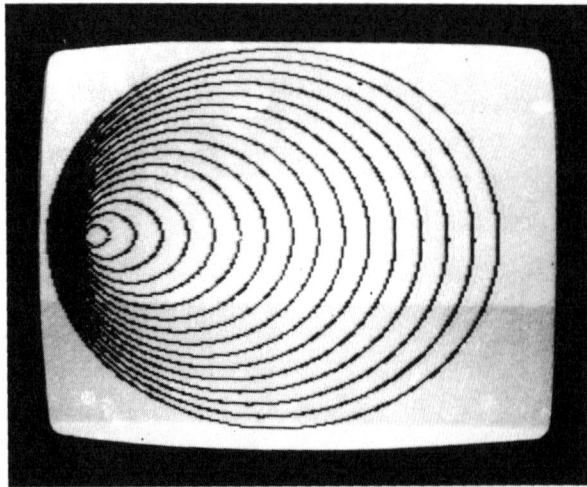

Figure 25.7   . . . Subsonic ones don't.

To see what happens at subsonic speed, change line 40 to:

40   CIRCLE 1.2 * C, .1

At the sound barrier itself, the transition between the two, the circles all pile up. Try:

40   CIRCLE C, 1

Ignore the error messages here.

CHAIN MAIL

Another nice demonstration draws a rectangular array of circles, like links in chain mail.

10   HIRES
20   FOR C = 30 TO 210 STEP 10
30   FOR R = 30 TO 170 STEP 10
40   CURSET C, R, 0
50   CIRCLE 5, 1
60   NEXT R
70   NEXT C

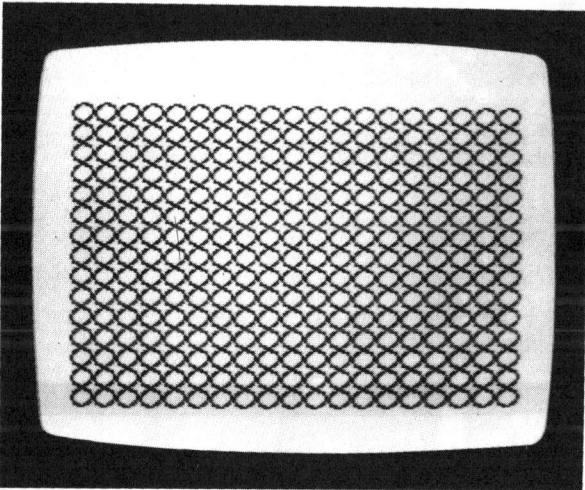

Figure 25.8   Chain Mail, radius 5.

Edit line 50 to CIRCLE 3, 1; to CIRCLE 7, 1; and to CIRCLE 20, 1 for other effects.

Project 3

Add a line 15 to the above program, so that you can input the radius of the circles, and modify line 50 accordingly. (Note: keep the radius below 30. Can you mug-trap to ensure this?)

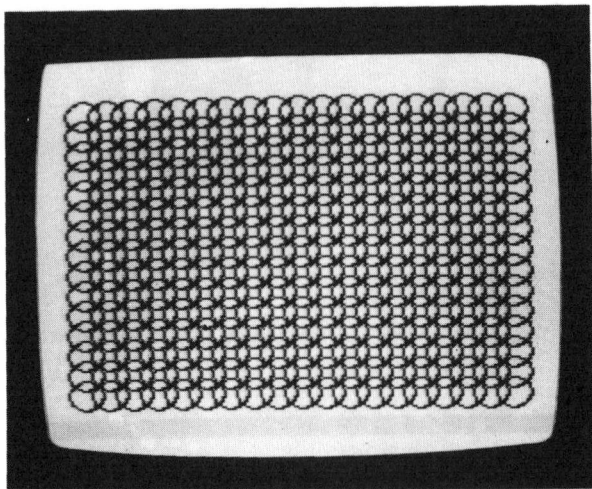

Figure 25.9   Chain Mail, radius 8.

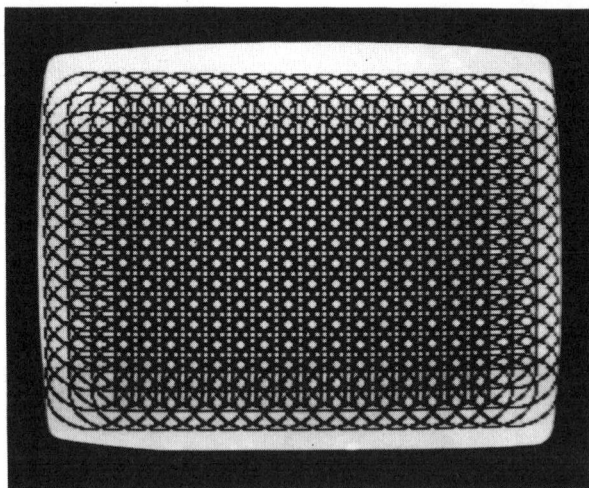

Figure 25.10   Chain Mail, radius 19.

DOTTED LINES

By using the command:

PATTERN

you can draw dotted lines. Rather than say too much, let me offer a test program:

```
10  HIRES
20  INPUT P
30  PATTERN P
```

```
40   FOR R = 20 TO 180 STEP 10
50   CURSET 20, R, 1
60   DRAW 200, 0, 1
70   NEXT R
80   FOR C = 20 TO 220 STEP 10
90   CURSET C, 20, 1
100  DRAW 0, 160, 1
110  NEXT C
```

The input P should be between 0 and 255 (0 produces blanks). You get dotted lines: the pattern of dots is like the 1s in the binary expansion of P, so you can use Appendix E of the *Manual.* In particular:

P = 60   gives long dashes.
P = 51   gives medium dashes.
P = 170   gives dots.

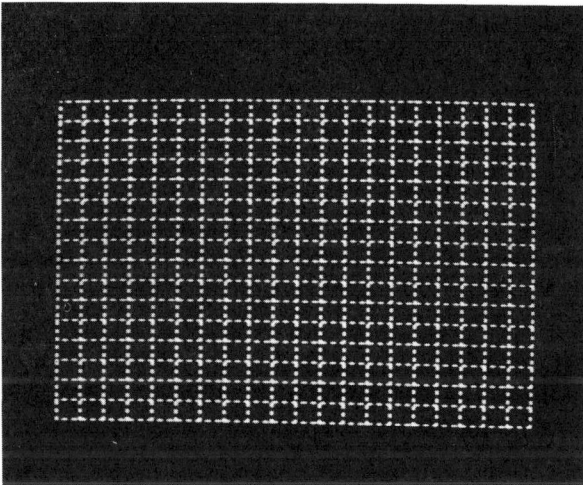

Figure 25.11   PATTERN used on a grid, giving dotted lines vertically and horizontally.

Project 4

How does PATTERN affect CIRCLEs? Write a test program to see.

Here are two more PATTERN programs: try them out. The second requires an input between 0 and 255.

```
10   HIRES
20   CURSET 120, 100, 0
30   FOR W = 1 TO 95
40   PATTERN W
50   CIRCLE W, 1
60   NEXT W
```

133

```
10    HIRES
20    INPUT P
30    PATTERN P
40    CURSET 120, 100, 0
50    FOR W = 1 TO 95
60    CIRCLE W, 1
70    NEXT W
```

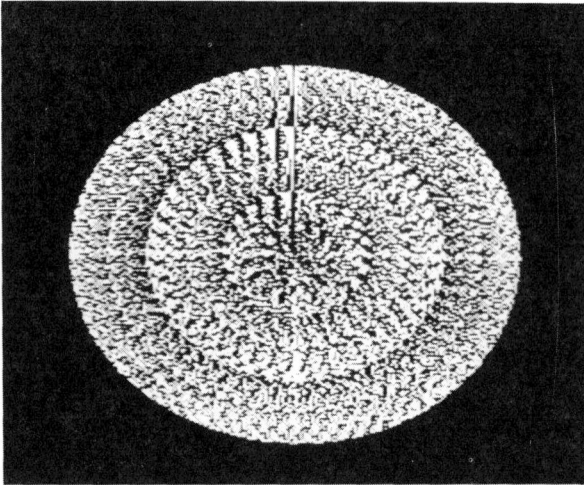

Figure 25.12   Circles formed by varying the PATTERN, assembled to give a disc.

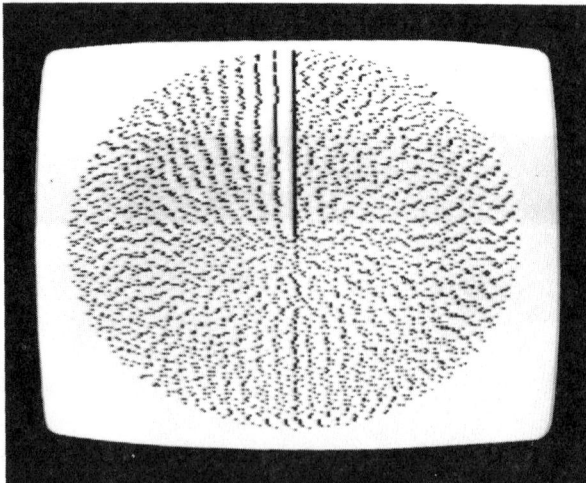

Figure 25.13   Circles with a fixed PATTERN.

ANSWERS

Project 1

```
 10  HIRES
 20  CURSET 120, 25, 1
 30  DRAW 80, 75, 1
 40  DRAW −80, 75, 1
 50  DRAW −80, −75, 1
 60  DRAW 80, −75, 1
 70  CURMOV 0, 25, 0
 80  DRAW 60, 50, 1
 90  DRAW −60, 50, 1
100  DRAW −60, −50, 1
110  DRAW 60, −50, 1
```

Project 2

```
 10  HIRES
 20  CURSET 120, 100, 0
 30  FOR W = 5 TO 50 STEP 5
 40  CIRCLE W, 1
 50  NEXT W
```

Project 3

Add:

```
 15  INPUT W
 50  CIRCLE W, 1
```

And to mug-trap:

```
 12  REPEAT
 17  UNTIL W > = 1 AND W < 30
```

Project 4

Much as it does for lines, working round the edge of the circle.

```
 10  HIRES
 20  INPUT P
 30  PATTERN P
 40  CURSET 120, 100, 0
 50  CIRCLE 50, 1
```

The Oric can be made to produce intricate multi-coloured displays in High-resolution; but you must learn how to poke the attributes to the screen.

26 Colour in High-resolution

Hi-res colour is controlled in essentially the same way as Lo-res colour: by the use of attributes. INK and PAPER work as usual (but you may lose whatever you've plotted in the first two screen columns). To *mix* colours on the Hi-res screen you can't use PLOT; instead you must POKE the correct memory location with the necessary attribute code. This technique is called 'Poking to the Screen' and should not be confused with what my son does when he's playing computer games: *his* version leaves sticky fingerprints all over the front of the TV.

HIGH-RESOLUTION ATTRIBUTE CONTROL

To set the scene, key this little program in:

```
10   HIRES
20   FOR R = 0 TO 199
30   FOR C = 0 TO 39
40   POKE 40960 + 40 * R + C, 16 + 8 * RND(1)     (POKE 8192 . . . for 16K)
50   NEXT C
60   NEXT R
```

It takes a few minutes: make the tea while you're waiting.

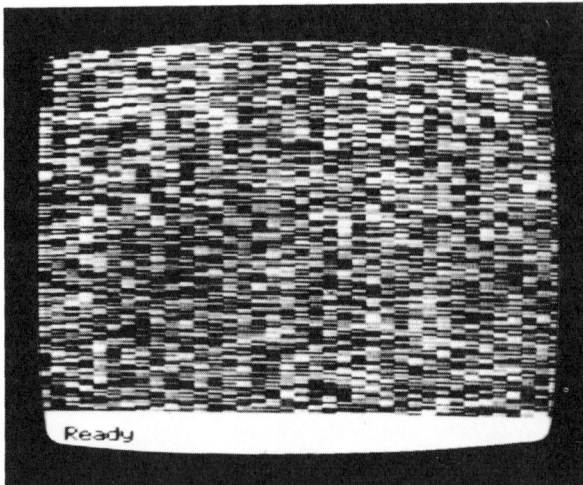

Figure 26.1   Random colours at the finest resolution possible, illustrating the structure of the Hi-res attributes.

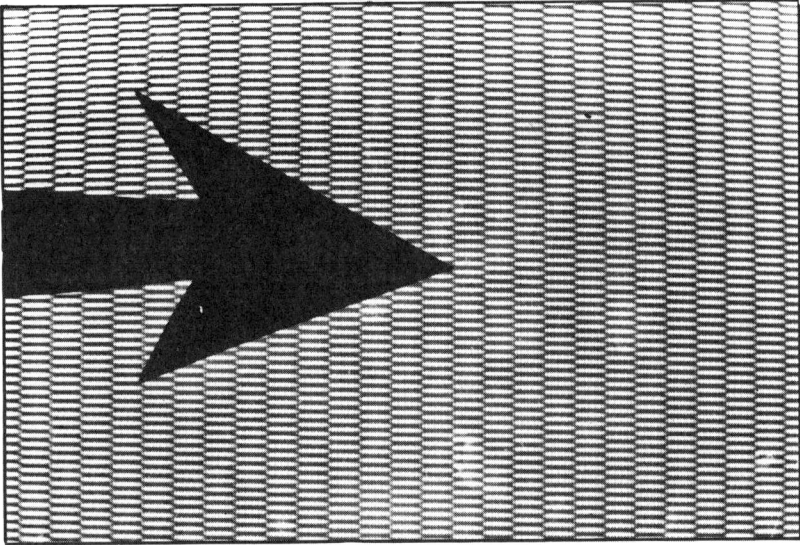

Figure 26.2 The structure of the Hi-res attribute file as seen on the TV display. The arrow is at the left-hand end of one tiny 1 × 6 cell, 'containing' exactly one attribute code.

If you thought that was pretty, interchange lines 20 and 30, and also 50 and 60, and have another go.

What's going on is this: the program is setting serial attributes, just as in LORES, and indeed using the same attribute numbers (here PAPER colours, attributes 16–23). *But:*

1. The cells to which the attributes apply are differently shaped.
2. You can't use PLOT to set an attribute: you have to 'POKE to the screen' as in line 40 of the program.

Look closely at the screen, with the above display sitting on it. You'll see that the coloured patches form short horizontal lines. The lines are actually six Hi-res cells long, and one cell high. In fact each 6 × 8 Lo-res cell has been sliced like a loaf into eight 6 × 1 Hi-res cells, as in Figure 26.3.

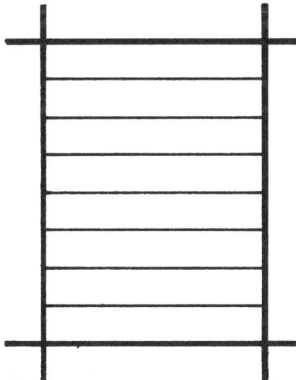

Figure 26.3 How a Lo-res cell divides into 8 Hi-res attribute cells.

These cells are stored in memory in the obvious order: Hi-res row 0 from left to right, 40 cells in all; then row 1, then row 2, . . . and so on in blocks of 40 until we reach row 199 and stop. See Figure 26.4 for a vague indication of what this looks like.

137

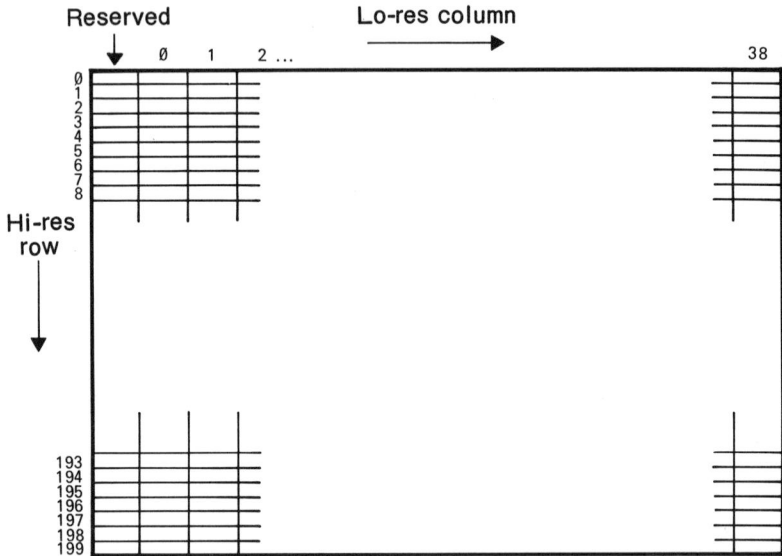

Figure 26.4   Structure of the Hi-res screen for POKEing attributes.

The address for the start of the Hi-res screen is:

40960   (8192 on a 16K machine)

and the addresses for the cells run like this:

		(reserved)	Ø	1		38
Hi-res	Ø	40960	40961	40962	. . .	40999
row	1	41000	41001	41002	. . .	41039
number	2	41040	41041	41042	. . .	41079
	.					
	.			....		
	.					
	199	48920	48921	48922	. . .	48959

Lo-res column number ⟶

(Subtract 32768 from these addresses for the 16K machine.) The attributes are again *serial,* that is, affect the *whole* of the row that follows them, until another attribute occurs. To set up an attribute whose code number is A at screen position R (Hi-res row) and C(Lo-res column) you must use:

POKE 40960 + 40 * R + C + 1, A   (POKE 8192 + . . . in 16K)

and to send it to the reserved column in row R, use:

POKE 40960 + 40 * R, A   (POKE 8192 + . . . 16K)

Think of these as Hi-res substitutes for the PLOT X, Y, A command in TEXT mode (Chapter 12). It's a slight nuisance having to think of the *rows* in Hi-res and the *columns* in Lo-res. If you're planning a colourful Hi-res display, using lots of CURSETs and such, don't forget that each attribute cell is 6 Hi-res cells long. That is, Lo-res column C runs from Hi-res position 6 * C + 1 to 6 * C + 6. Confused? So am I; so Figure 26.5 shows what part of the Hi-res screen looks like when we want to draw a diagonal line in red ink on a screen whose normal ink colour is yellow. See what's going on? It's just like Cyril the squirrel, but sliced finely in the vertical direction.

Attribute 1

Attribute 1

Attribute 1

Attribute 1

Attribute 1

Attribute 1

Attribute 1

Attribute 1

Yellow

Red

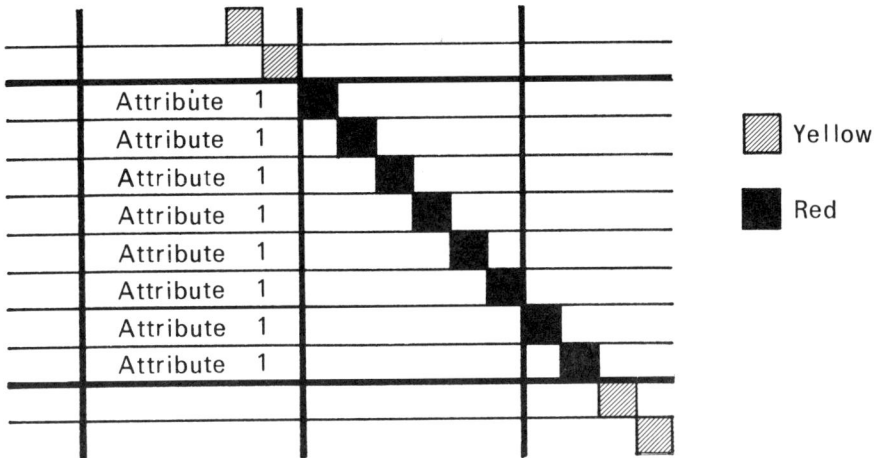

Figure 26.5 Effect of red INK attributes (code 1) on a Hi-res line, assuming yellow INK has been set globally. Just like Lo-res attributes, but sliced thinly in the vertical direction only.

EXAMPLES

A couple of examples will demonstrate some of the possibilities. The first lets you see all the main attributes in action.

```
10   HIRES
20   A = 0
30   FOR R = 0 TO 199
40   AD = 40960 + 40 * R          (AD = 8192 + 40 * R in 16K)
50   IF R = 8 * INT(R/8) THEN A = A + 1
60   IF A > 23 THEN A = 23
70   POKE AD, A
80   NEXT R
90   FOR C = 0 TO 20
100  CURSET C, 0, 0
110  DRAW 200, 199, 1
120  NEXT C
```

This POKEs attributes 0–23 into the reserved column of screen, eight rows at a time; then the diagonal band draws something so that you can see the effect. The next program is similar, but puts random INK attributes (0–7) into the reserved column:

```
10   HIRES
20   FOR R = 0 TO 199
30   POKE 40960 + 40 * R, 8 * RND(1)     (POKE 8192 . . . in 16K)
40   NEXT R
50   FOR C = 0 TO 20
60   CURSET C, 0, 0
70   DRAW 200, 199, 1
80   NEXT C
```

Project 1

Use serial attributes to draw a solid circle in the centre of the screen, radius 20, whose top half is red and whose bottom half is green.

CHARACTERS IN HIGH-RESOLUTION

It is possible to print ordinary characters on to the Hi-res screen, one at a time, by using the command:

CHAR

In fact, the syntax for this is:

CHAR N, S, K

where N is the ASCII code of the character you want, S is Ø for the standard set, 1 for the alternate set, and K is Ø for PAPER colour, 1 for INK. The character is printed with its top left corner at the position of the Hi-res cursor. So you need two steps again:

1. Set the cursor with CURSET or CURMOV.
2. Use CHAR to get what you want.

I'm running out of space, so here's a quick demonstration of the power of this command:

```
10   HIRES
20   FOR C = 1 TO 230
30   CURSET C - 1, 100, 0
40   CHAR 65, 0, 0
50   CURMOV 1, 0, 0
60   CHAR 65, 0, 1
70   NEXT C
```

LISSAJOUS CATALOGUE

Finally, multicoloured graph-plotting, showing what can be achieved by attention to detail. (The individual curves could be plotted in a more sophisticated way, but it's the colour control that I want you to see.)

```
 9   REM SET UP ATTRIBUTES
10   HIRES
20   FOR A = 0 TO 2
30   FOR B = 0 TO 3
40   COL = 4 * A + B + 1
50   IF COL > 7 THEN COL = COL - 7
60   FOR R = 0 TO 59
70   POKE 40960 + 40 * (R + 60 * A) + 10 * B, COL        (8192 in 16K)
80   NEXT R
90   NEXT B
100  NEXT A
```

```
199   REM PLOT LISSAJOUS FIGURES
200   FOR A = 0 TO 2
210   FOR B = 0 TO 3
220   A0 = 60 * A + 30
230   B0 = 60 * B + 30
240   CURSET B0, A0, 0
250   FOR T = 0 TO 2 * PI STEP .03
260   X = 20 * SIN(A * T + T + 1)
270   Y = 20 * COS(B * T + T)
280   CURMOV X, Y, 1
290   CURSET B0, A0, 0
300   NEXT T
310   NEXT B
320   NEXT A
399   REM TITLE MESSAGE
400   M$ = "LISSAJOUS FIGURES"
410   FOR Z = 1 TO LEN(M$)
420   Q$ = MID$(M$, Z, 1)
430   K = ASC(Q$)
440   CURSET 50 + 8 * Z, 188, 0
450   CHAR K, 0, 1
460   NEXT Z
470   STOP
```

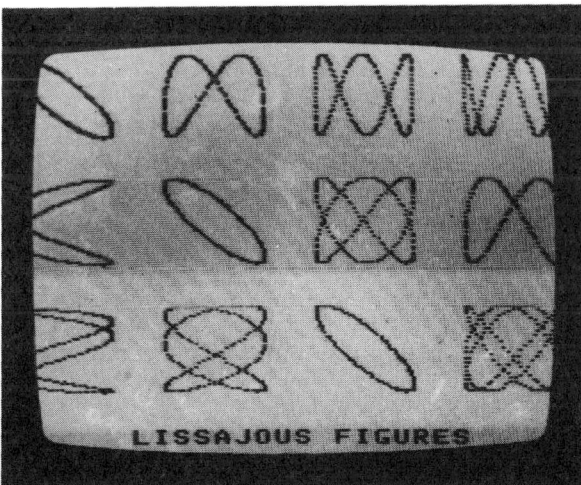

Figure 26.6 Lissajous Figures, composed of two independent oscillations. The program plots them in different INK colours on a black screen. The photo is in black-and-white for clarity.

141

I'm not going to attempt to explain what's going on: there's a complicated interplay between Lo-res and Hi-res numbering systems. But observe the end effect: different coloured curves on different parts of the screen.

Warning The computer takes a minute or so to set up the attributes, during which time you just see a black screen. And the whole program takes several more minutes to draw the curves. But it's worth waiting for!

ANSWER

Project 1

```
 10   HIRES
 20   FOR R = 0 TO 99
 30   POKE 40960 + 40 * R, 1     (8192 in 16K)
 40   NEXT R
 50   FOR R = 100 TO 199
 60   POKE 40960 + 40 * R, 2     (8192 in 16K)
 70   NEXT R
100   CURSET 120, 100, 1
110   FOR W = 1 TO 20
120   CIRCLE W, 1
130   NEXT W
```

27 Debugging V

How do we prove conclusively that a program does precisely what it was written to do? I don't want to get involved in too complicated a philosophical discussion (because that's where we are headed) but, broadly, it's a bit like asking an astronomer whether the sun will rise tomorrow. If he is very pedantic he might answer that the earth has been going round the sun for a long time now and we have a body of physical laws which suggest that it will continue to do so in a regular way, and that the smart money would be on this continuing to be the case tomorrow; but he would add that he has no way of knowing whether our physical laws are right and that what we have observed for thousands of years might in fact be a manifestation of a much more complex law whose effect, tomorrow, might be to reverse the direction of the earth's rotation or to take it out of orbit completely.

DORMANT BUGS

By analogy, because a program behaves correctly for the first thousand sets of data input to it, there's no absolute guarantee that it will work for the thousand and first. In fact, bugs often don't become apparent until months or even years after a program has been apparently successfully completed and has been run without problems dozens or even hundreds of times. This isn't really surprising; after all, it's the conditions which occur least often that the programmer is most likely to overlook.

Here's an example:

We are writing a suite of programs for the Nether Hopping Electricity Board to handle their customer accounts. They explain to us that there are two tariffs, A and B. On the A tariff the consumer pays a quarterly standing charge of £15 and then pays for units used at a rate of 4p per unit. On the B tariff the consumer pays no standing charge and pays 7p per unit. So we write a piece of code like:

```
100   INPUT T$
105   INPUT UNITS
110   IF T$ = "A" THEN 300
120   IF T$ = "B" THEN 140
130   GOTO 5000
140   BILL = 7 * UNITS/100
150   PRINT BILL
160   GOTO 100
300   BILL = 15 + 4 * UNITS/100
```

```
310   PRINT BILL
320   GOTO 100

      . . .

5000  PRINT "INVALID TARIFF"
5010  STOP
```

OK. I know the code could be more efficient, and that we would actually need some more information like the consumer's name and account number, but you get the basic idea.

So we test this piece of code and it works fine and we go away muttering that it is a waste of our remarkable talents to be given Noddy programs like that to write.

And it does work fine; for years; and then one day it prints a bill for £0.00. Of course, nobody notices because it's one of thousands of bills and anyway it's probably enveloped automatically. The recipient is puzzled and probably amused by the bill because it shows how stupid computers are but there seems no point in taking any action so he throws the bill away. Unfortunately, we wrote another program in the same suite which stores the date that each bill was despatched, and if it does not receive confirmation that the bill has been paid within 28 days, it prints a final demand notice. This time the recipient is more irritated than amused but he just consigns it to the waste paper basket, as before. At this point things start to go visibly wrong. The routine which checks the delay between presentation of the account and payment issues an order to the maintenance department to cut off the consumer when he still hasn't paid after 60 days.

What's happened? Easy!! The consumer is an old-age pensioner who has taken advantage of one of the long winter break packages that the travel companies offer to senior citizens. He was out of the country for just over three months and used no electricity in a full account period. He is also an unusually frugal user of electricity so he's on tariff B. That's why the system printed out a request for zero payment, and of course it won't happen very often because very few people will be away from home for that long, and tariff B users are likely to be thin on the ground, too. For the problem to occur, the consumer has to fit both conditions.

Once seen, the bug is easily squashed:

```
145   IF BILL = 0 THEN 100
```

so that the PRINT statement is avoided. This problem is supposed to have occurred in an early computer system, although whether it's a folk tale I wouldn't like to say. In any event, I think it illustrates neatly how a bug can lie dormant almost indefinitely.

The moral is: when you invent data to test a program, don't do so at random. Choose values at and close to branch values in the program. If a statement says:

```
305   IF U < 30 THEN 400
```

then run a test with U at 29.999 and another at U = 30 and another at U = 30.0001. You may have meant:

```
305   IF U < = 30 THEN 400
```

If you only test at U = 15 and U = 160 you won't notice the error.

Make sure test data have been chosen so that every section of the program gets executed at some time. And of course, make sure you know exactly what the answer should be for each set of test data.

*If you feel like a change of
character, a little bit of
POKEing in the right place
works wonders . . .*

28 User-defined Characters

If you don't like Oric's character set—or, more likely, if you want to use a special character in a program, that's not in either the standard or alternate set—then you can redefine *any* character to suit your taste.

First you design your character, on a 6 × 8 grid, like Figure 28.1 Go along each row, and when you hit a black square, add in the number at the top of that column. Write the result on the right-hand side, as I've done.

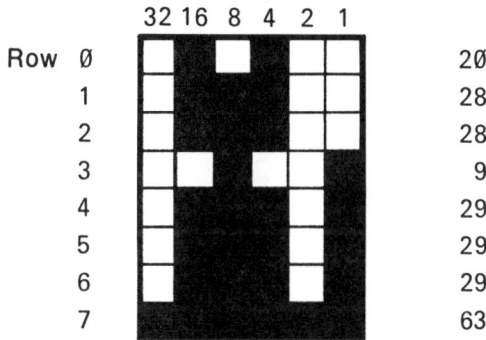

*Figure 28.1   User-defined cat character. The numerical data for each row are read off by
summing the numbers above black squares.*

For instance, row 2 goes like this: there are blocks in columns 16, 8, 4; add to give 28. (Alternatively write '1' for a black square, '0' for a blank, and convert from binary to decimal using Appendix E of the *Manual*.)

Now we need to shove these numbers into memory, where the codes for the character we want to redefine usually live. I'm going to give you a standard program to do this, which you can incorporate into any program that needs a user-defined character. It uses the commands DATA and READ which we met in Chapter 7.

```
10   DATA 20, 28, 28, 9, 29, 29, 29, 63
20   C$ = "@"
30   AD = 46080 + 8 * ASC (C$)              (AD = 13312 . . . in 16K)
40   RESTORE
50   FOR T = 0 TO 7
60   READ X
70   POKE AD + T, X
80   NEXT T
100  PRINT "HERE IT IS:"; C$
```

RUN this: you'll find that your selected character '@' has now acquired feline characteristics. It will stay that way until you turn off the current, RESET, or redefine it yet again.

To use this for a different character, replace '@' by whatever you fancy; and for a different design, replace the DATA list by your new numbers.

Project 1

Set up character 'A' to be the box in Figure 28.2.

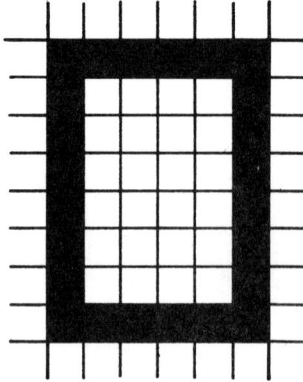

Figure 28.2   Box to be produced in Project 1.

Project 2

Design a rocket shape, and set up 'R' to produce it.

CHARACTER BUILDER

The *Manual* (page 89) gives you a (somewhat perverse) program to enter data numerically, and thereby redefine a chosen character. I'm going to go one better, and let you design the character, large scale, on the screen. The rest is automatic.

```
  9  REM INITIALIZE
 10  CLS
 20  DIM K(6, 8)
 30  DIM N(8)

 99  REM PLOT DOTS
100  FOR T = 0 TO 5
110  FOR U = 0 TO 7
120  PLOT 10 + T, 10 + U, "."
130  NEXT U
140  NEXT T

199  REM DESIGN
200  FOR T = 0 TO 5
210  FOR U = 0 TO 7
```

```
220   PLOT 10 + T, 10 + U, "?"
230   GET A$
240   IF A$ = "0" THEN PLOT 10 + T, 10 + U, "▽"
250   IF A$ = "1" THEN PLOT 10 + T, 10 + U, CHR$ (126)
260   K(T, U) = VAL(A$)
270   NEXT U
280   NEXT T

299   REM CORRECTION FACILITY
300   PLOT 5, 8, "IS THIS RIGHT?"
310   GET Q$
320   IF Q$ = "N" THEN PLOT 5, 8, "▽▽▽▽▽▽▽▽▽▽▽▽▽▽": GOTO 200

399   REM SET UP CHARACTER DATA
400   INPUT "WHICH CHARACTER"; C$
410   FOR U = 0 TO 7
420   N = 0
430   FOR T = 0 TO 5
440   IF K(T, U) = 1 THEN N = N + 2 ↑ (5 − T)
450   NEXT T
460   N(U) = N
470   NEXT U

499   REM LIST CHARACTER DATA
500   FOR U = 0 TO 7
510   PRINT N(U);
520   NEXT U
530   PRINT

599   REM POKE DATA TO CHARACTER SET
600   AD = 46080 + 8 * ASC(C$)          (AD = 13312 . . . in 16K)
610   FOR U = 0 TO 7
620   POKE AD + U, N(U)
630   NEXT U

699   REM PRINT SAMPLE
700   PRINT "THIS IS HOW IT LOOKS"; C$
710   STOP
```

When you RUN this, you'll see a 6×8 array of dots and a '?'. If you hit key '0' the ? disappears, if you hit '1' you get a shaded block. The cursor '?' moves on down the first column, then the second, and so on until you've covered the entire array of dots.

Now you get a chance to change things. The message 'IS THIS RIGHT?' appears. If you press key 'N' you get another go: note that you must again run right through the whole array, but that the old blocks remain until the '?' cursor reaches them. (This actually helps you work out where to make changes.)

Press anything except 'N' and the computer now asks you to decide which character is to be redefined, does so, prints out the data for the eight rows in case you want to make a record of them, and displays a sample of the new character, actual size.

Project 3

See how Character Builder works on the cat, Figure 28.1.

ANSWERS

Project 1

Edit '@' to 'A' and change the DATA list to:

63, 33, 33, 33, 33, 33, 33, 63

Project 2

If your rocket is like Figure 28.3, you'll need to edit '@' to 'R' and the DATA list to:

8, 8, 28, 28, 28, 28, 54, 34

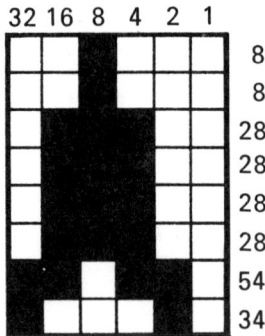

Figure 28.3   Rocket shape for Project 2.

Project 3

There isn't an answer: you just have to *do* it.

A powerful programming technique allows you to break a program down into a series of identifiable subtasks, which can be designed one at a time and then linked together:

29 Subroutines

Often a particular sequence of commands gets used several times within a program. You *may* be able to avoid writing the sequence several times by judicious use of GOTO commands; but this isn't always good enough. The command:

GOSUB

is like a GOTO that 'remembers where it came from'. On meeting another command:

RETURN

the program jumps back to the line *after* the particular GOSUB line that it originally started from.

For instance, Chapter 7 gives a standard procedure for producing input messages at the top of the screen and wiping them out afterwards, to keep everything tidy. It's a nuisance writing this for *every* occasion an input is required. Here's a way to avoid this. First we work out the *subroutine* we need in *general* form. We then need to print some prompt PROMPT$ and input, say, a string I$; after which we erase the prompt. This can be done by:

```
100   PLOT 1, 0, PROMPT$
110   PRINT CHR$(30)
120   INPUT I$
130   PRINT CHR$(30)
140   PRINT SPC(38)
150   RETURN
```

Now we write the rest of the program. Suppose it has to ask for your first name and surname, and then print out the whole thing. Then you add these lines:

```
 5   CLS
10   PROMPT$ = "SURNAME"
20   GOSUB 100
30   SUR$ = I$
40   PROMPT$ = "FIRST NAME"
50   GOSUB 100
60   FIR$ = I$
70   PRINT "YOUR FULL NAME IS"
80   PRINT FIR$; "∇"; SUR$
90   STOP
```

Line 20 *calls* the subroutine, having set PROMPT$ to SURNAME. The subroutine itself then asks for that, inputs your answer as I$, and wipes out the message: RETURN *sends it to line* 30, immediately after this GOSUB. It now sets PROMPT$ to FIRST NAME, and repeats the process; but on the next RETURN it goes instead to line 60, the one after *that* GOSUB. See how much more useful this is than a GOTO? Meanwhile line 30 has remembered the first input I$ under the name SUR$, which leaves I$ free for the next call of the subroutine. (If you didn't do this, the second call would just change the original surname input to the new first name input: not what you want at all.) Line 90 stops you running into the subroutine again.

Project 1

Write a subroutine that lets you input a character and a row number. Then add program lines that call this routine *twice*, so that you end up with (say) row 3 full of Xs and row 7 full of Ws—assuming you input X, 3 first time and W, 7 the next.

FRUIT MACHINE

This program uses a subroutine to produce a rudimentary fruit-machine game. The subroutine prints out a block of characters in an arbitrary position: the program calls this three times to get the complete display.

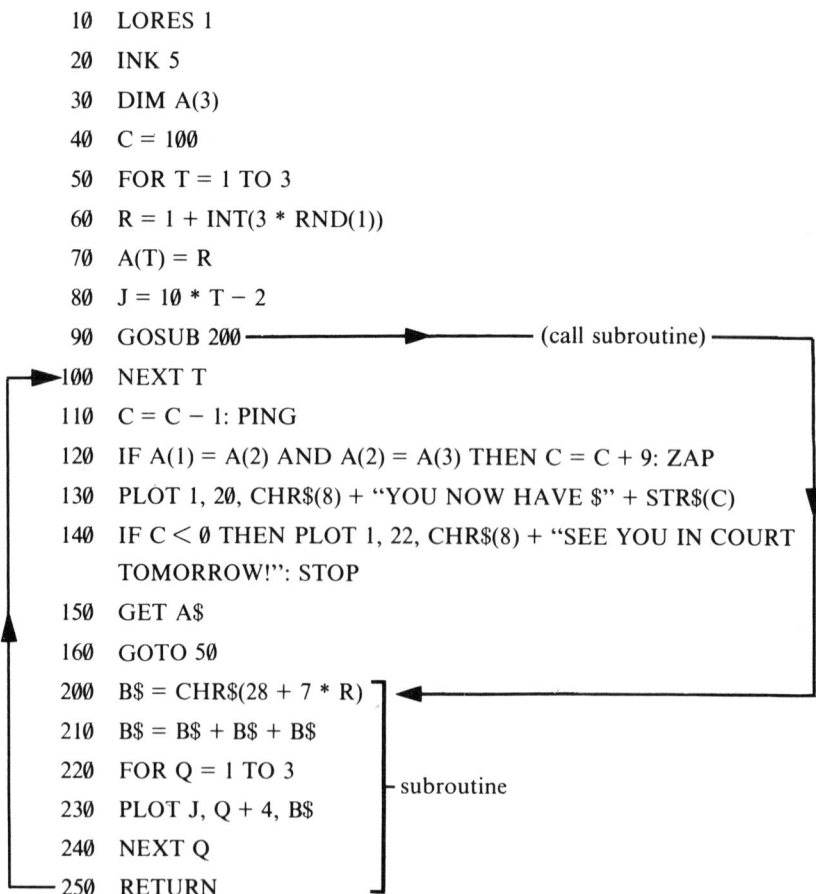

```
 10   LORES 1
 20   INK 5
 30   DIM A(3)
 40   C = 100
 50   FOR T = 1 TO 3
 60   R = 1 + INT(3 * RND(1))
 70   A(T) = R
 80   J = 10 * T - 2
 90   GOSUB 200 ————————————————————— (call subroutine) ——————
100   NEXT T
110   C = C - 1: PING
120   IF A(1) = A(2) AND A(2) = A(3) THEN C = C + 9: ZAP
130   PLOT 1, 20, CHR$(8) + "YOU NOW HAVE $" + STR$(C)
140   IF C < 0 THEN PLOT 1, 22, CHR$(8) + "SEE YOU IN COURT
      TOMORROW!": STOP
150   GET A$
160   GOTO 50
200   B$ = CHR$(28 + 7 * R)
210   B$ = B$ + B$ + B$
220   FOR Q = 1 TO 3                  } subroutine
230   PLOT J, Q + 4, B$
240   NEXT Q
250   RETURN
```

If you run this, you get another turn every time you press a key. The subroutine draws three magenta patterns. If these are the same, you win $8. If not, you lose $1. You start with $100 and can keep going until you lose the lot (which takes *ages*, because the odds are fair).

There's some initial setting up in lines 10–40. Lines 50–100 set up a loop which selects a random pattern, calls a subroutine to draw it, and repeats twice more.

Line 110 deducts your stake; line 120 computes your winnings.

Line 130 tells you how much cash you now have. Note the use of CHR$(8) to return to standard characters, and STR$(C) to convert C to a string for printing. Line 140 works the same way, when you run out of cash.

Line 150 just waits for a key-press, and 160 repeats the whole process again for your next go.

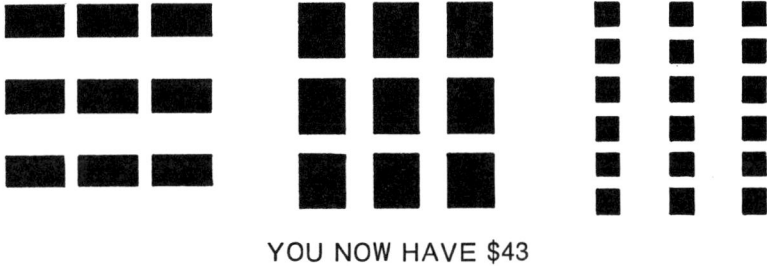

YOU NOW HAVE $43

Figure 29.1 Typical Fruit Machine display, formed by plotting alternate characters in suitable blocks.

Project 2

Modify the program so that if you press key 'S', the program stops.

You can call (use GOSUB with reference to) a subroutine from within another subroutine if you wish: Oric will sort out which RETURN goes where.

STRUCTURED PROGRAMMING

There's another important use of subroutines: they let you design a program in bite-sized chunks, a process known as *top-down* programming. The structure of such a program is relatively easy to see from a listing. There's not space to go into this at length; but I'll illustrate the idea on the 'Cyril the Squirrel' program.

To 'top-down' Cyril, I'd *start* writing the program like this. (I've chosen the line numbers to avoid making too many changes: if I'd *really* started this way I would probably have put the main program at the front.)

```
 999   REM MAIN STEPS IN PROGRAM
1000   GOSUB 10: REM INITIALIZE
1010   GOSUB 100: REM COLUMN OF NUTS
1020   GOSUB 200: REM DISPLAY CYRIL
1030   IF RND(1) > .95 THEN GOSUB 300: REM
       DROP A NUT WITH 1 IN 20 CHANCE
1040   GOSUB 400: REM KEYBOARD SCAN
1050   GOSUB 600: REM SEARCH FOR NUTS
1060   IF T > 0 THEN 1020: REM T = NUT TOTAL
1070   GOSUB 800: REM TIE UP ENDING
1080   STOP
```

The general flow of the program is perfectly clear; but I haven't yet tackled any of the details. This illustrates Jones's First Law of Computing: *never put off till tomorrow what you can put off till the day after.* It's what top-downing is all about.

Only now do I tackle the subroutines themselves. They're nearly all like the corresponding bits of the original Cyril program (and I'll use the same line numbers, see Chapter 20), except that I must add RETURNs in lines 60, 130, 230, 350, 510, 650. I've done the RND(1) > .95 test already, in line 1030, so I'd delete line 300 (and renumber 310–350 as 300–340, otherwise Oric wouldn't let me jump to 300—or I could put in a dummy 300 REM instead).

Line 1060 takes care of what line 700 did before; and I'm left with one final subroutine:

```
799   REM: TIE UP ENDING
800   PLOT 1, 1, CHR$(8) + "WELL DONE CYRIL!"
810   PRINT CHR$(6)
820   INK 0
830   RETURN
```

Now I'm all ready to run (using GOTO 1000 to start in the right place!) with the minimum of effort. Moreover, I can debug the subroutines individually (by setting up suitable test conditions), and if one doesn't work, I can pull it out and put a different one in. And other modifications are just as easy. Suppose instead of the ZAP in line 620, I want the computer to play 'Waltzing Matilda' whenever Cyril finds a nut. Then I cross out the ZAP and replace it with:

```
GOSUB 2000
```

(say), and then all I've got to work out is what happens between:

```
1999   REM WALTZING MATILDA
2000   ????????
        . . .
2400   RETURN
```

That's your job: it's not a million miles away from 'Jesu, Joy of Man's Desiring' as far as the *program* goes, so you can use the ideas in Chapter 22. You don't expect me to do *everything,* surely? Anyway, are you *certain* you want a squirrel that plays *Waltzing Matilda?*

ANSWERS

Project 1

Here's the subroutine:

```
1000   INPUT "CHARACTER"; C$
1010   INPUT "NUMBER"; N
1020   RETURN
```

Now the main program:

```
10   DIM B$(2), M(2)
20   FOR K = 1 TO 2
30   GOSUB 1000
40   B$(K) = C$: M(K) = N
```

```
 50  NEXT K
 60  CLS
 70  FOR K = 1 TO 2
 80  FOR C = 1 TO 38
 90  PLOT C, M(K), B$(K)
100  NEXT C
110  NEXT K
120  STOP
```

Project 2

This isn't about subroutines: it's about your ability to understand the flow of control in a program. The simplest solution is to add:

155 IF A$ = "S" THEN STOP

because that's where (a) you input information, and (b) decide to have another go. It is, so to speak, the weak link in the chain of command.

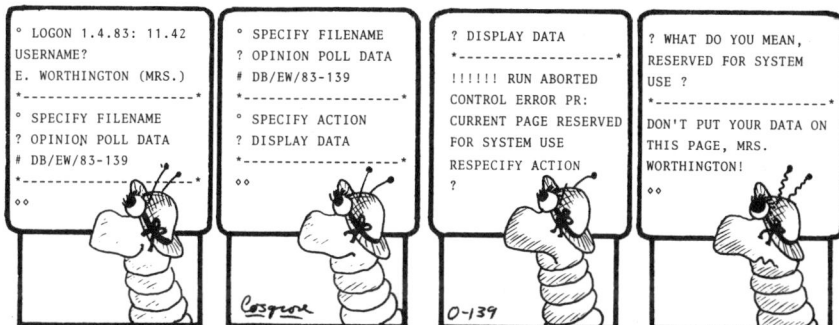

```
° LOGON 1.4.83: 11.42
USERNAME?
E. WORTHINGTON (MRS.)
*---------------------*
° SPECIFY FILENAME
? OPINION POLL DATA
# DB/EW/83-139
*---------------------*
◦◦
```

```
° SPECIFY FILENAME
? OPINION POLL DATA
# DB/EW/83-139
*---------------------*
° SPECIFY ACTION
? DISPLAY DATA
*---------------------*
◦◦
```

```
? DISPLAY DATA
*---------------------*
!!!!!! RUN ABORTED
CONTROL ERROR PR:
CURRENT PAGE RESERVED
FOR SYSTEM USE
RESPECIFY ACTION
?
```

```
? WHAT DO YOU MEAN,
RESERVED FOR SYSTEM
USE ?
*---------------------*
DON'T PUT YOUR DATA ON
THIS PAGE, MRS.
WORTHINGTON!
◦◦
```

153

30 Debugging VI

ROUND-OFF ERRORS

The kinds of bugs we've looked at so far have been of our own making, and have been reasonably easy to cure once we have seen them. There's another kind of bug which is caused by the design of the machine itself. It's not a design fault but a consquence of the way all computers are organized. It's to do with the precision with which computers store numbers. If we think about any common way of holding numbers it's obvious that there is a limit to the number of digits that can be held. A car mileometer, for example, can only hold 5 digits because it only has 5 'windows'. It's just the same with a computer. Each number can occupy no more than fixed number of 'windows'. However, each window does not represent a decimal digit. The internal machine code for numbers is quite different from the way we think about them, and I will not bore you with the gory details. The fact that there is inherent inaccuracy *and* a code conversion being employed means that the external representation of a number (as it is displayed on the screen) may not be quite the same thing as the internal representation. I'll give you an example of what I'm talking about from school logarithms. If you multiply 2 by 2 using logs you get:

No.	Log.
2	0.3010
2	0.3010
3.999	0.6020 +

i.e. $2 \times 2 = 3.999$!!

The combination of the fact that the logs are only accurate to 4 figures (i.e. they are only allowed to occupy 4 windows) and that a code conversion (number to logarithm, logarithm back to number) is taking place, creates the inaccuracy.

Here's a program which causes the same kind of problem:

```
10   FOR P = 1 TO 10
20   S = SQR(P)
30   Q = S * S
40   IF P < > Q THEN PRINT P, Q
50   NEXT P
```

Take the case where $P = 9$. At line 20 it is square rooted, so $S = 3$. We then square S at line 30, so $Q = 9$, the same as P. Of course, P will always equal Q because the operation of square rooting followed by squaring is bound to get you back where you started. So line 40 is silly, because P is never different from Q and nothing will be printed.

Or is it? Try running the program. You get:

5	5
6	6.00000001
7	7
9	9

This is a very strange result indeed, because the machine is not only printing out values, and so claiming they are different, but it is also printing them as if they were the same! What has happened is that the complex mathematical processes involved have led to slight inaccuracies in the internal representation of the numbers, which have accounted for the differences between P and Q. However, there are *also* inaccuracies involved in decoding the internal format back to the decimal numbers displayed on the screen so that they *appear* to be identical although the machine is adamant that they are not. For some values the internal codes are identical—8, for instance.

This kind of error can be extremely puzzling and sometimes the only way out is to allow a small error in the IF statement so that we have:

IF ABS(P − Q) < 0.0001 THEN . . .

The ABS function is necessary because Q might be greater than P, in which case the result would be negative and so less than 0.0001, although its value could be very large. (− 30 is less than 0.0001!) The ABS chops off the minus sign.

Round-off errors are especially common if you use T↑N for N^{th} powers of whole numbers T (see the *Manual* page 20). Try this:

```
10   FOR T = 1 TO 10
20   PRINT T * T, T↑2
30   NEXT T
```

If you want, say, the fifth power of a whole number T, it's better to use:

T * T * T * T * T

and not:

T↑5

as far as accuracy goes. In fact T↑N is calculated as:

EXP(N * LN(T))

(for those who know about logarithms and exponentials).

This isn't the end: it's just the beginning. The question is:

31 What Next?

Even if this book has now exhausted you, you haven't exhausted your Oric. On the contrary, you've only scratched the surface—there are several commands that I haven't had room to mention at all. So here are a few suggestions for getting a bit more out of the machine:

1. This may sound obvious, but read the *Manual* again. You'll find that it makes a lot more sense than it did first time through. That's not because this is such a marvellous book that it's opened your eyes to the Rich Panorama of Computing: it's just that, like most worthwhile things, progress gets easier after you've made the initial effort. The more you know already, the easier it is to appreciate new ideas.
2. I've said nothing at all about add-ons like the *teletext communications Modem.*
3. At the time of writing, the Oric is so new that there are hardly any specialist publications—books and magazines. No doubt that will soon change, so keep your eyes open. You can learn a lot of useful tricks from even short programs. A good general computer magazine is *Personal Computer World,* and *Popular Computing Weekly* is inexpensive and covers a wide range of machines. *Oric Owner* magazine is available from Tansoft, 3 Club Mews, Ely, Cambs.
4. Don't assume that unless a program has been written specifically for the Oric, it's no use. You can often modify programs intended for other machines (though specialist features like PEEK and POKE or graphics characters can lead to extensive re-thinks). For example, many programs written for the ZX81, ZX Spectrum, or Dragon will run on an Oric with minor changes, of which the main ones are:

   (a) Different codes (and shapes) for graphics characters.
   (b) LET is compulsory on ZXs but can be omitted on Orics.
   (c) GOTO is compulsory on ZXs in IF . . . THEN . . . GOTO commands.
   (d) PRINT AT X, Y on ZXs, or PRINT@ 32 * X + Y on Dragons become (roughly) PLOT Y,X,1 on an Oric.
   (e) LINE on a Dragon corresponds roughly to DRAW on an Oric.
   (f) PLOT X, Y on a Spectrum, or PSET X, Y on a Dragon, translate as CURSET X, Y, 1 on an Oric. And Spectrum graphics come out upside down, so CURSET X, 199 − Y, 1 may be needed.
   (g) The syntax varies in annoying but basically routine ways.
   (h) Colour and sound are pains in the neck: the three machines use totally different systems.

   The trick is to understand what the program is trying to do in a given line, and work out how an Oric might do it.
5. *Tapes* for most other machines will *not* run on an Oric: stick to the range that is specifically intended for it.

6. In most areas there are now computer clubs and user-groups which you can join for moral support and material assistance. Look in your local newspaper, ask the local school, or consult computer magazines.
7. As well as BASIC, the Oric can also work in Machine Code, via the command USR. This is not exactly *advanced*—in a sense it's very rudimentary—but you have to take care of all the nuts-and-bolts tasks that BASIC does automatically. This means more work for you, but often leads to faster-running programs. See page 123 of the *Manual,* if you really want to use Machine Code. The magazines often carry short Machine Code routines that you can use without having to wade through all the theory.
8. You're on your own now. Good luck!

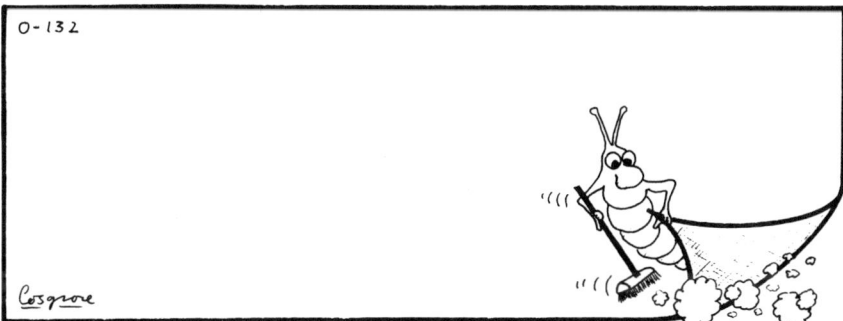

O-132

Cosgrove

Appendix I: Control Characters

Key	ASCII[1]	Effect
CTRL/A	1	Edit mode: puts screen characters into buffer
CTRL/B	2	
CTRL/C	3	Break: interrupt program run
*CTRL/D	**4**	Auto double height: print on two lines
CTRL/E	5	
*CTRL/F	**6**	Keyclick on/off
CTRL/G	**7**	Ping
CTRL/H	(**8**)	Cursor left[2]
CTRL/I	(**9**)	Cursor right[2]
CTRL/J	10	Cursor down
CTRL/K	11	Cursor up
CTRL/L	**12**	Clear screen and reset cursor to top left (CLS)
CTRL/M	13	Carriage return: cursor to left and down one row
CTRL/N	14	Clear row, leave cursor in position
*CTRL/O	15	Disable cursor movement and keyboard input
*CTRL/P	16	Printer
*CTRL/Q	**17**	Cursor on/off
CTRL/R	18	
*CTRL/S	**19**	Screen display disable/enable
*CTRL/T	**20**	CAPS lock
CTRL/U	21	
CTRL/V	22	
CTRL/W	23	
CTRL/X	24	Line delete, plots backslash \
CTRL/Y	25	
CTRL/Z	**26**	Allows attributes to be sent to cursor position[3]
CTRL/[	**27**	Allows attributes to be sent to cursor position[3]
CTRL/\	28	
*CTRL/]	**29**	Access to protected column (far left)
	30	Clear cursor to top left, leave screen[4]

Notes

1. Boldface ASCII codes are sometimes useful in programs, accessed by PRINT CHR$(code).
2. In LORES modes, CHR$(8) and CHR$(9) switch between standard and alternate character sets.
3. Position cursor, type CTRL/Z or CTRL/[. Now keys A, B, C, . . . send attributes 1, 2, 3, . . . to cursor position (although first two columns work differently in TEXT or LORES mode and the attribute affects only one cell in LORES).
4. Not accessible from keyboard.
* Toggle action (one press for *on*, next press *off*, and so on).

Appendix 2: Alternate Character Set

Block Graphics Characters (32–95, 160–233)

Characters with codes between 32 and 95 are shown: adding 128 produces inverse video (ink and paper interchanged). Corresponding standard characters are shown.

Alt.	ASCII	Std.	Alt.	ASCII	Std.	Alt.	ASCII	Std.	Alt.	ASCII	Std.
▦	32	space	▦	48	0	▦	64	@	▦	80	P
▦	33	!	▦	49	1	▦	65	A	▦	81	Q
▦	34	"	▦	50	2	▦	66	B	▦	82	R
▦	35	#	▦	51	3	▦	67	C	▦	83	S
▦	36	$	▦	52	4	▦	68	D	▦	84	T
▦	37	%	▦	53	5	▦	69	E	▦	85	U
▦	38	&	▦	54	6	▦	70	F	▦	86	V
▦	39	′	▦	55	7	▦	71	G	▦	87	W
▦	40	(	▦	56	8	▦	72	H	▦	88	X
▦	41	)	▦	57	9	▦	73	I	▦	89	Y
▦	42	*	▦	58	:	▦	74	J	▦	90	Z
▦	43	+	▦	59	;	▦	75	K	▦	91	[
▦	44	,	▦	60	<	▦	76	L	▦	92	\
▦	45	–	▦	61	=	▦	77	M	▦	93	]
▦	46	.	▦	62	>	▦	78	N	▦	94	↑
▦	47	/	▦	63	?	▦	79	O	▦	95	£

Attributes (0–31, 128–159)

0–31   Usual attribute effect.

128–159   Complementary attribute: colour code C becomes 7 −C (e.g. green becomes magenta).

Special Teletext Characters (96–127, 224–255)

96 - 111

112 - 115

116

117,122,127

118 - 121,123 - 126

Adding 128 inverts.

Program Index

Commands and Symbols Index

Other titles of interest

Games to Play on your Oric-1 £4.95
Czes Kosniowski

Programming for REAL Beginners £2.95
Philip Crookall

Brainteasers for BASIC Computers £4.95
Gordon Lee

**PEEK, POKE, BYTE & RAM! Basic Programming
for the ZX81** £4.95
Ian Stewart & Robin Jones

'Far and away the best book for ZX81 users new to
computing'—*Popular Computing Weekly*

' . . . the best introduction to using this trail blazing micro'—
Computers in Schools

'One of fifty books already published on the Sinclair micros, it is
the best introduction accessible to all computing novices'—
Laboratory Equipment Digest

Machine Code and better Basic £7.50
Ian Stewart & Robin Jones

' . . . a beautifully written course in so-called advanced
programming, concentrating on program structuring, data-
handling and machine coding'—*Education Equipment*

The ZX81 Add-On Book £5.50
Martin Wren-Hilton

Easy Programming for the ZX Spectrum £5.95
Ian Stewart & Robin Jones

' . . . will take you a long way into the mysteries of the Spectrum: is
written with a consistent and humorous hand: and shares the
affection the authors feel for the computer'—*ZX Computing*

Further Programming for the ZX Spectrum £5.95
Ian Stewart & Robin Jones

Spectrum Machine Code £5.25
Ian Stewart & Robin Jones

Computer Puzzles: For Spectrum and ZX81 £2.50
Ian Stewart & Robin Jones

'What a gem of a book!'—*Education Equipment*

Games to Play on Your ZX Spectrum £1.95
Martin Wren-Hilton

Spectrum in Education £6.50
Eric Deeson

Easy Programming for the Dragon 32   **£5.95**
Ian Stewart & Robin Jones

Further Programming for the Dragon 32   **£5.95**
Ian Stewart & Robin Jones

Easy Programming for the BBC Micro   **£5.95**
Eric Deeson

Further Programming for the BBC Micro   **£5.95**
Alan Thomas

BBC Micro Assembly Language   **£7.95**
Bruce Smith

BBC Micro in Education   **£6.50**
Eric Deeson

Shiva Software

Spectrum Special 1   **£5.95**
Ian Stewart & Robin Jones
A selection of 10 educational games and puzzles.

Spectrum Specials 2 & 3   **£5.95 each**
Ian Stewart & Robin Jones

Shiva Educational Software available late '83

Please write for details

Plus more to come!